The Happy End
of Comedy

Jonson, Molière, and Shakespeare

The Happy End of Comedy

Jonson, Molière, and Shakespeare

Zvi Jagendorf

Newark: University of Delaware Press
London and Toronto: Associated University Presses

Associated University Presses
440 Forsgate Drive
Cranbury, NJ 08512

Associated University Presses
25 Sicilian Avenue
London WC1A 2QH, England

Associated University Presses
2133 Royal Windsor Drive
Unit 1
Mississauga, Ontario
Canada L5J 1K5

Library of Congress Cataloging in Publication Data

Jagendorf, Zvi, 1936–
  The happy end of comedy.

  Bibliography: p.
  Includes index.
  1. Comedy—History and criticism.   2. Closure
(Rhetoric)   3. Shakespeare, William, 1564–1616—Comedies.
4. Jonson, Ben, 1573?–1637—Comedies.   5. Molière,
1622–1673—Criticism and interpretation.   I. Title.
PN1929.C5J3   1984   822'.0523'09   83-40238
ISBN 0-87413-239-8

Printed in the United States of America

Most of Chapter 1 appeared as an essay in *Hebrew University Studies in Literature* (Autumn 1978). I am grateful to the editors for their permission to reprint this material.

2265849

For Malka

Contents

1   A Theoretical Introduction to the Study of Ending in
    Comedy   11
2   How Comedies End   33
3   Perplexing the Catastrophe: Endings in Jonson's Comedy   44
4   Molière's Denouements   78
5   Patterns of Resolution in Shakespeare's Comedies   111
Notes   162
Select Bibliography   171
Index   175

1

A Theoretical Introduction to the Study of Ending in Comedy

> *Pat! he comes, like the catastrophe of the old comedy.*
> —*King Lear*

A study of comic endings is really a study of the mode itself. Clearly enough, the ending of any work of art that can be said to have a beginning and an end is an organic part of an aesthetic whole, and isolating it for study would seem artificial. However, the strategy of ending is a legitimate subject for aesthetic discourse,[1] the aim of which is not to isolate the end of a work arbitrarily but rather to observe the ways in which the artist molds the conventional necessity of ending to fit the burden and movement of the work as it has developed.

Nowhere is convention, the formal model, more obviously present than at the ending of a novel, play, poem, or piece of music. Traditionally, the artist, especially in the oral mode, has had recourse to quite obvious signals of the approaching end. The couplet at the end of a Shakespearean sonnet, the careful accounting of fates and disposing of fortunes at the end of a Victorian novel, the recognition motif at the end of New Comedy, and the "they lived happily ever after" of the children's tale—all these use an obvious formal device to emphasize finality. That these so often blunt endings sometimes achieve their formal purpose without necessarily "completing" the work—that is, answering all the questions that it has raised or settling all the conflicts and tensions it has enacted—is notorious.[2] There is necessarily a strained relationship between the subtlety and myriad insights in the work as it unfolds to the eye or to the imagination and formulas of ending that would put a stop to irony and arouse suspicion by their stock-in-trade finality. This may be a peculiarly modern unease. Modern writers have gone out of their way to avoid the rhetorical end.

Beckett's dramas end where they began *in medias res,* and Joyce ends *Ulysses* at a high point in Molly's reverie, which is arrested in full flow by the white expanse of the unprinted space. Here the end is an interruption rather than a formally announced completion, and Molly's life is allowed to sail on into the Dublin night, as *we* leave the scene.

Also in the theater we leave the scene, but usually after a final tableau of pronounced formality. Like the other performing arts, the theater concentrates unusual attention on the sequence of ending (it is the signal for applause, after all). It is this sequence that juxtaposes in time the make-believe of the spectacle and the spectator's return to himself and the everyday. The tension between the two experiences, present whenever we confront a fiction, is magnified by the presence of an audience in a theater before live actors who are in their role one moment and out of it the next.

In comedy the return to ordinary experience may be guided wittily by the actor who drops his mask, by the clever or moral epilogue, or by the direct call for applause. The final sequence itself, so often a tour de force of quick changes, sudden revelations, surprising confrontations, not only unties all the knots, but draws the spectator's attention to the artistry of both poet and performer. So often at the end of comedies skill is on display. We are invited directly or by inference to look at the bare bones out of which the play was made, to accept consciously the unashamed artificiality of its conventions, and yet to admit their success in creating briefly a spectacle that engaged us in a different, more serious way. Comic endings are in themselves a convention, an agreement between poet and spectator rather than a necessary outcome of the material.[3] Within the framework of the larger convention numerous lesser but familiar devices are used to bring about the happy end. Yet comic plots do often deal with material that does not lend itself easily to comic solutions. Obsessions are obstinate, self-delusion is deeply rooted, and ingrained folly is incurable. The devices and displayed skills of the ending, then, tend to deal in a pronouncedly artificial way with passions, fixations, and relationships that resist the conventions created to master them. This kind of clash between convention and material is characteristic of comedy and emerges as a complicating factor, disturbing the smooth symmetries of denouement.

The nature of the ending has been a subject for theoretical and practical discussion throughout the history of the criticism of tragedy and comedy.[4] Both major kinds of drama are to be differentiated, among other things, by their endings, and Aristotle classifies the kinds of endings that are appropriate to each. His mention of the comic ending is by way of example in a discussion of the best tragic ending. In this discussion he prefers the Euripidean model of the catastrophic ending to the mixed ending that serves up two kinds of fate, one for the good and one for the bad. This mixed ending, he finds, occurs when the poet writes to serve "the wishes of his audience" and it produces a pleasure akin to that of comedy. The example of a comic ending in this passage is one "where those who, in the piece, are the deadliest enemies—like Orestes and Aegisthus—quit the stage as friends at the close and no one slays or is slain."[5]

Aristotle's brief remarks here hint at some of the major differences in the characteristic structures and subject matter of tragedy and comedy, differences that will help us throw light on the formal nature of the comic end.

Tragedy's end is determined by a necessity that is inherent in the fable to begin with, and made intelligible by the poet through his manipulation of character and action. Everything that happens on the tragic stage is measured by this principle of necessity, this truth which looms larger and larger until it is displayed in all its clarity in the catastrophic ending. This principle severely limits the poet's freedom of invention. If his tragedy is to achieve its required pitch of sublimity, if it is to convince us that the action set out on the stage is binding as a paradigm, and not simply another *fait divers,* then every facet of the plot, every gesture—indeed, every thought and word of the charac-ters—must be marked with the tragic purpose. Thus the very human and touching action of the shepherd listening to the cry of the infant Oedipus and having mercy on him is both a totally natural action and a link in the necessary chain that binds the baby's birth to his errors and exile. The tragic art is an art of limitation. The tragic artist analyzes experience in the name of a principle that he and his audience accept as real and binding. The necessary end of tragedy, is, then, palpably present in its beginning as the Ghost lurks in Elsinore and the plague takes its toll of the citizens of Thebes.

If the tragic poet subjects man's desire to the limitations of reality, the comic poet changes experience in accordance with the demands of desire. The internal necessity reflecting an objective truth that deter-mines the shape of tragedy has no corollary in comedy, where anything can happen. It is rather the absence of this necessity that characterizes the comic mode. Fundamentally, the end of comedy is determined by no objective structural principle, only a conventional one. You must have a happy ending.[6] The simplest structure of the comic plot is that of accumulation, the accumulation of incident, word, and action all serv-ing the principle of pleasure-giving and creating. The characteristic hero of such a plot is the type of figure that is capable of spinning out of himself a seemingly endless variety of comic language and gesture: the Falstaff, the nimble fool, the clownish buffoon, the wit, the target of wit, and the indestructible Punch. Such figures and the plots they inhabit need owe no allegiance to anything outside the obvious fiction that experience conforms to desire. Thus Aristotle can in his example point to the arbitrary nature of the comic plot. The poet may twist the given facts of experience to suit himself, his unserious characters, and the desire of his audience. No one is killed, and the worst of enemies leave the stage arm-in-arm. However, the pleasure-giving principle that informs comedy is neither really independent nor free of the limitations imposed by man's mortal nature. At some point this principle, which allows the accumulation of pleasure-giving speech and action, encounters, and even arouses, forces that oppose it. Indeed, it may be said to bear the seeds of its own defeat.

The rhythm of pleasure-creating is a climbing rhythm, pushing on toward exhaustion or excess, rather than fulfillment. The urge is to enact ever more preposterous tricks until either a breakdown or a violent climax is likely.[7] Here the independent pleasure-loving comic principle meets with the sanctions of a social reality outside the world of gratified pleasure. Horace in his miniature history of comedy, in the *Epistle to Augustus,*[8] tells of the banning of the Fescennine revels because they had gone too far in the direction of riot. This example from the primitive Italian agricultural carnival holds true of the thematics of more sophisticated comedy. The fiction of arbitrariness and independence of a sober reality is sustainable only up to a point. Comic characters may act as if there is no nemesis, comic plots may twist action into the most preposterous shapes of accident and coincidence, the impulse to change experience to conform with desire may be the driving impulse of the comic hero, yet the shadow of sober reality, even of mortality, cannot be banished. The preposterous end of Aristotle's example, like the wittily preposterous end of *The Beggar's Opera,*[9] is not necessarily a victory for pleasure over necessity. Rather it is the parading of a fiction at a point where that fiction is most fragile. That seems to happen with the endings of many comedies.

Before turning to the relation between the ending of comedy and the conflicts that animate it, one could ask whether it is possible to construct a model of the emotional state of the spectator at the end of a comedy, as Aristotle did for the spectator of tragedy. In what mood is the spectator thought to leave the theater after watching a spectacle of the ridiculous? Plato, at least in the *Republic,* considered the likely state of mind to be conducive to undignified and shameful behavior. The spectator will go home and imitate the degrading antics of the buffoon.[10] According to this familiar view, the experience of seeing comedy rather aggravates than tames man's innate tendency to behave irresponsibly. There is no artistic control and the sensations aroused by the freedom of the riotous comic spectacle mingle destructively with the delicate system of rational and emotional responses necessary to cope with everyday life. A classic defense against this change is to be found, among other places, in Sir Philip Sidney's *Apology for Poetry*. ". . . comedy is an imitation of the common errors of our life, which he representeth in the most ridiculous and scornful sort that may be; so as it is impossible that any beholder can be content to be such a one."[11] Sidney in his desire to protect poets from charges of moral subversiveness, posits a very simple model of the interaction between the spectacle and spectator in comedy. This spectacle makes no attempt to elicit feelings other than those of scornful rejection. The obviousness of the comic mask and the transparency of the comic plot make it impossible for more complicated feelings to appear. Thus the ridiculous comic target exhausts those feelings that it was created to arouse, and a simple balance is achieved.

Both examples are extremist and partial accounts of a state of mind that may be created by the comic experience. They rule out the possibility of a subtlety of response, of a manipulation and formulation of varied feeling through character and plot, similar at least in complexity to the way in which the tragic writer brings his audience to accept the conclusion of his drama.

In a tragic play the strong, man-centered feelings aroused by the spectacle of suffering encounter the nonhuman principle of truth, which informs the play. Our pity for Lear or for Hamlet has to face the inexorable in their predicaments, and the feeling is disciplined by what we perceive to be real. Comic plots may also arouse strong sensations, whether it is delight at the wit of the nimble trickster, mockery of the absurd fool, or pity for the lost and entangled lovers. But they are not so well equipped to mediate between these sensations and the world to which the spectator returns. This is because the comic ending is founded on no objective principle the truth of which puts everything else into perspective. Comic endings are rather solutions, exploiting social institutions such as marriage, courts of law, identification parades, and banquets for the façade of finality that they provide. The efficacy of such a solution depends to some extent on the nature of the sensations aroused by the play in its career. The stronger and more varied these have been, the more we will expect of the ending.

What models can be suggested for the relationship between the varied emotions aroused by a comedy and the conventional formulations of its end? One view put forward in a neo-Aristotelian study of comedy[12] is that the comic plot proves to us that any concern we felt for the characters in their predicaments was groundless and absurd. Comedy, therefore, aims at a relaxation of concern, and a neutralization of emotion in laughter. According to this analysis the comic poet in dealing with his material drains it of the kind of seriousness that encourages the spectator to respond with strong or complicated feeling. Thus even the most arbitrary of endings appropriately crowns the unserious action. All dissolves in laughter.

This model resembles Sidney's definition in that it invests the comic action with the mechanical efficiency of a simple structure created to elicit a simple response. As a theoretical framework it seems to deny those qualities in comedy that are positive rather than negative. The pleasure and delight it assumes comedy to afford are based on a static relationship between the spectator and the spectacle. The unimportance of the comic action signaled to us by means of conventions of speech, character, stage gesture, and plot frees us, according to this view, of the burden of complexity and conflict in our reaction. Our laughter is a continual sign of our superior status to the antics of the comedians.

This approach may be in line with Aristotle's idea that the comic is a form of the ugly, the harmlessly ugly, and that the comic figure is unlike us in his ridiculous postures and predicaments.[13] However, its assumption of the lack of real emotional claim in comedy seems wrong, whether it is *Lysistrata, Twelfth Night, Volpone,* or *Tartuffe* we are talking about.

At the very origin of the impulse to create in the comic mode there is an emotional commitment by the artist and performer that is not touched upon in Aristotelian theory. The comic artist is as much a celebrant of man's unideal personality and abnormalities as he is a critic and judge of his failure to order his life according to social norms. In his role as judge the comic poet will make use of devices that isolate and label his object. The conventional mask or stereotype is such a device and its emotional appeal is circumscribed by its familiarity and by the obviousness with which it declares its nature. In his role as celebrant, however, the comic poet delights in those traits that deviate from norms of morality or of beauty. This is the source of much comic gusto, of the characteristic love of detail in comic speech, and the unashamed self-display of even the most monstrous comic characters. In the hands of the celebrant the conventions transcend themselves, and the mask that, from one point of view is limited in its emotional appeal, derives amazing power and energy from the very narrowness of its conception. Mosca is no "town flatterer." He is the parasite per se. Molière's obsessed characters are paragons of obsession; their mental prison may be a harmful one, but it is so well documented that we outside become fascinated with its logic and moved by its demonic strength.

Volpone, Argan, and Falstaff play very different roles in plays that do not have very much in common; but in each case the figure engages the spectator's concern in such a way that the judgment, arrangement or solution of the end appears questionable rather than convincing, more ironic than stable. In these cases the outcome has not made us regard the emotions we invested in the characters as absurd. The opposite has occurred; the emotions provoked by the characters and their predicaments have made the outcome *itself* unsatisfactory, and sometimes absurd. In each case and in different ways a conflict has been created between the specifically comic vitality of a character and the return to the norm. This tension is not only based on character, though it is easy to point it out there. It is often present when a comedy engages us on a more than primitive level and it suggests that the social poise and emotional balance that the formal endings seem to dramatize are not necessarily the serene way out of the comic imbroglio that they appear to be. Indeed, they may provide a façade for a less civilized energy, libidinous, unruly, abnormal, and self-centered, which is suppressed but not overcome. If the comic end does achieve stasis, it is only by allowing expression to those attitudes such as the above that would upset it. It is often the continued presence of sex, gluttony, melancholy, and even the shadow of death that gives the happy end some resilience and authority.

The rhythmic pattern is similar. As comic plots near their end they tend to accelerate rather than subside in rhythm, seemingly heading toward an enactment of uncontrolled riot or unbearable deadlock. Both in simple farces like *The Comedy of Errors* and in elaborately constructed works like *Volpone* and *Twelfth Night,* the twists and turns of plot become remarkably pronounced as the end approaches. This frenzied movement in an ever-shrinking space, as the lines of the plot converge, creates in the spectator a parallel upsurge of excitement that the formal ceremony of the closing scene can hardly quell. Giddiness and riot are rarely far away from the harmony that ends many of Shakespeare's comedies, Jonson's judges and honest men put the lid on practices that have infected them, while Aristophanes' exits are full-scale explosions of merry-making and song and (in *The Clouds*) even of violence.

When in *An Essay of Dramatic Poesy* Dryden's Eugenius talks about denouement, he refers to it as "things settling again upon their first foundations."[14] Eugenius is a conservative. For him the ideal plot is circular. Its catastrophe makes for a return to a settled, normal state of affairs, presumed to have existed before the spectacle of error and confusion took over the stage. This return is made possible by the removal of those "obstacles which hinder the design" and it creates assent by its "resemblance of truth and nature." Eugenius's model of an ending is perhaps the one most commonly accepted when we think of comedy. The very design and pattern of the plot, maintained in spite of disturbing obstacles, contain the promise of a satisfactory outcome. Confusion is only a seeming disturbance on a soundly symmetrical base. Erring twins are bound to discover each other and oddly arranged pairs of lovers must by the end have arranged themselves harmoniously. However, the denouement of the comic plot does not always produce a return only to a preexisting norm. A different emphasis would posit the creation of a new situation at the end, fostered by the struggles and confusions of the main action.[15] If one model implies the achievement of balance within accepted norms of behavior, the other entertains the possibility of change and of a reappraisal of norms of behavior exhibited in the play. Most comic endings move between these two possibilities, and often contain features of both. Balance has to be reconciled with the ingrained disequilibrium of much comic matter, and conversions and recognition of folly must confront the dramatically powerful recalcitrance of both fool and knave.

Indeed, it is possible to construct models of the different types of happy endings by considering the kinds of struggle or disequilibrium that they have to resolve. Like all things in drama, comic endings are reached through struggle. The critical tradition, beginning with Aristotle, and the post-classical commentators on Terence expressed this struggle in terms of the metaphor of tying and untying,[16] or more specifically to comedy, the rhetorical triad of protasis, epitasis, and catastrophe (the growing action, the height of bustle, and the sudden turn of events).[17] These traditional categories are derived, both in the case of Aristotle and that of Donatus, from observation and from the empirical analysis of the plays in question. They describe a peculiar dramatic structure and infer an ideal form from it. But although their emphasis is anatomical, on the skeletal and spatial arrangement of a comedy rather than on its movement, their terms do focus attention on the kinds of underlying conflict that make happy endings a challenge.

To achieve ending, the writer of comedy has to modulate the kinds of energy that complicate and push the action to its climax into situations that lend themselves to the kind of closure the mode leads his audience to expect. The problem peculiar to comedy is that the kinds of energy that go into creating the climax do not easily lend themselves to the modulations of the closing convention. One might summarize the relation between middle and ending action in comedy in terms parallel to those of the early commentators, though with a modern bias towards the way the manipulation of feeling characterizes a literary form. If we replace Aristotle's *desis* or "tying" with the idea of deadlock and Donatus's *epitasis* which he called "stormy"[18] with the idea of riot, we may formulate the problem of ending thus: somehow an acceptable happy ending must be accomplished, although both deadlock and riot, for different reasons, will not let it happen.

On the surface riot and deadlock are polar opposites. They certainly represent different strategies of feeling. Riot is the wild, violent, amoral, and anarchic core out of which much comic action grows, beckoning the spectator to take pleasure in its excess. Its rhythm is a mounting rhythm, pushing forward toward frenzy (Donatus's stormy epitasis). Its logical fulfillment is the state of being out of control. Its most graphic physical expression on the stage is the dizzying chase of bodies, teetering on the edge of imbalance that one finds in the climactic moments of farce and in the increasingly violent blundering of Shakespeare's pairs of lovers and twins in *A Midsummer Night's Dream* and *The Comedy of Errors*. Deadlock, which is the high point of Aristotle's tying action, is in terms of feeling quite simply the denial of fulfillment, usually to the natural and legitimate desires of central characters such as young lovers. But more generally it may be thought of as the principle in the play that plots against all movement and change. It is approximate to a base kind of reality principle, that of the deniers of wit, the jealous husbands, and the avaricious fathers. Expressed in physical terms, deadlock is the aim of Gros-René, the surly servant in Molière's early farce, *Le Médecin volant*. Sganarelle, for love and wit's sake, is playing both a doctor and his brother. Gros-René is suspicious:

> Le diable emporte! ils ne sont qu'un.
> *(Le Médecin volant, 15)*[19]

and wants to catch him out. If he did, Sganarelle's nimble movement would stop, the young lovers would not get away, and there would be no happy end.

Both riot and deadlock are enemies of balanced resolution in comedy. The former is so because its logic of excess will not suit any ending short of an explosion or a giddy spinning; the latter, because its parsimony and hostility to all that is genial would block the victory of wit and love and freeze the action in the grip of some dour humor, malicious urge, or unlucky accident. Yet both features are often simultaneously present at the height of turbulence in comedies, creating the hysteria of absurd and irresponsible action that is the outer expression of deadlock. Thus when the lovers in *A Midsummer Night's Dream* and the twins of *The Comedy of Errors* run amok in their maze of forest and town, their violence of movement and language is the physical and verbal face of the state of being trapped. The riotous actions of chasing, beating, cursing, in fact push toward immobility—the exhaustion of sleep or the sanctuary of the Priory. Out of that immobility Shakespeare then spins his fabric of resolution.

Both riot and deadlock need to undergo some kind of modulation to make possible the release that produces an acceptable happy ending. This modulation—in other words, the denouement (Aristotle's lysis)— may be long or short, involve recognition by the major characters or leave them ignorant, emphasize its own artifice, or claim to be natural. All these choices depend on the nature and tradition of the particular comedy. But all comedies do, to some extent, embody the unruly impulse of riot and the latent immobility of deadlock, so thinking about the nature of denouement really has to confront the permutations of all three factors in the major comic categories.

What seems clear is that in comedies which take recognition seriously the process of denouement is elaborate, since the characters, including deluded and recalcitrant ones, are led to a point where they can become cognizant of what they have not known before. Those in which recognition is not an important factor in ending limit the untying action and deploy riot and deadlock as close to the end as possible. Here there is no need of a complex unraveling; quick, surprising end-stopping of the action is all that is needed.

Indeed, a typology of comic endings could be constructed according to the complexity and pathos of the denouement and the proximity or distance from it of riot and deadlock. The most primitive comic actions have no denouement to speak of; farce can have virtually none. At the other pole is romantic comedy as practiced by Shakespeare with its elaborate, often emotional unraveling, and its sophisticated emphasis on the mystery and artifice of that unraveling. Close to the simple actions are satires, which end abruptly in sudden revelation or through the intervention of a deus ex machina. Plays dominated by obsessed humor characters, like many of Molière's comedies, end logically, indeed inevitably with a trapped character sealing his own defeat (Alceste, Arnolphe) or more hopefully, his madness is adapted to the needs of the society around him *(Le Malade imaginaire.)*

The puppet play of Mr. Punch is a good example of the kind of comic action in which there is no denouement to speak of and certainly no recognition, but simply an interruption of the combination of riot and deadlock that reigns on the stage. The puppet Punch of the English tradition is an unambiguous figure of riot who is violent, selfish, and defiant of natural and human law. Deadlock here is both the human law, which would put him behind bars and hang him, and the metaphysical law, which would take him to Hell to encounter the Devil.

Mr. Punch is a primitive comic trickster, and as such he bears a charmed life rooted in the spectator's delight in his stylized aggression and expected maliciousness. The text of the play *The Dominion of Fancy, or, Punch's Opera* was noted down by Mayhew, the Victorian sociologist, from a wandering puppet master and published in his *London Labour and the London Poor.*[20]

Punch's career in this version of the play is composed of a series of encounters with "others," beginning with his own wife and child and ending with judges, hangmen, and Satan himself. In each encounter Punch pitches his wit or his selfish desire against the demands or intelligence of his antagonists, and in most of them, Punch's superior wit and violent energy engineer the downfall of his victim. Baby, wife, beadle, hangman—all exit dead or severely mauled, while Punch himself, ever-elastic, falls "dead" only once, to rebound at some cost to the doctor's nose. These encounters, in a plot that parodies crime and punishment, show how Punch evades responsibility consistently, proving himself in each situation to be the pleasure-giving monster that his audience wishes to see. His manipulator sums it up well when he describes the scene of Punch in prison for his crimes:

> Scene draws up, and discovers the exterior of a prison, with Punch peeping through the bars, and singing a merry song of the merry bells of England, all of the olden time. (That's an olden song, you know; it's old ancient, and it's a moral—a moral song, you know, to show that Punch is repenting, but pleased, and yet don't care nothink at all about it, for he's frolicsome, and on the height of his frolic and amusement to all the juveniles, old and young, rich and poor. We must put all classes together.)[21]

This kind of figure is invincible because he exists simply to gratify our childish desire for ever more tricks. That is why any civilized feeling he might display, such as regret or repentance, can only be a parody, a product of the frolicking that is his real raison d'être. Yet in the traditional puppet play this invincible trickster is brought face-to-face with Satan. According to the manipulator, Satan wants to take Punch away, for all his past misdeeds and frolic and fun, to the bottomless pit. Satan, then, comes as is his wont, to present the account and specifically in this case to equate wrong-doing and fun. His defeat in the climactic stick fight of the play is a victory of comic virtuosity over conventional responsibility, and it is a signal for imagined riot in the audience as well, as Punch and his manipulator seem to know: " 'Bravo! Hooray! Satan is dead,' he cries (we must have a good conclusion); 'we can now all do as we like!'—(That's the moral, you see.)"[22] Here is a primitive comic plot that dramatizes riot and license within the extreme stylization of the puppet theater and can conclude in no other way than by exhibiting the final triumph of riot on stage and as an option to the audience. This triumph is based on the consistency of the leading puppet, which in turn depends on the spectator's will to be entertained by such a caricature of humanity. The riotous end pays tribute above all to the resilience of the famous puppet, whose chastening or defeat would be totally unacceptable. This simple play, then, needs no strategy of ending. Despite his ironic lip service to morality, the manipulator knows that his spectacle is unambiguous; Punch's preposterous victory is present already in his swagger and the squeak of his voice as he first appears. Only in a theater of pure convention is such freedom possible.

It is also possible, or almost so in farce, where characters moved by various kinds of lubricity or dashing toward absurd goals race against an accelerating plot in a shrinking space.[23] Riot is present in the accelerating rhythm of speech and movement, in the accumulation of absurd objects, like the presents in René Clair's film *An Italian Straw Hat* and above all in the ever-present threat of irresponsible and explosive activity, like the beatings of the wrong man in *The Menaechmi,* and the Marx Brothers' descent upon *Il Trovatore* in *A Night at the Opera.* In farce, which is so dependent on nimbleness, exercised on the very edge of a chasm, deadlock is whatever threatens the freedom of the acrobats in their absurd race. Inopportune discovery, for instance, would bring the whole crazy structure down on the head of the poor bridegroom in *An Italian Straw Hat.* He would lose his bride and his presents, and the complicated activity of hours would result in nothing. Instead, the lucky discovery of an identical hat makes possible an ending that reimposes the fake bourgeois calm of marriage on the one hand and cuckoldry on the other.

Denouement, then, may be absent in farce because there is no call for a modulating action to intervene between madness and the end. Instead riot is pushed as close to the end as it will go until something interrupts, and makes an acceptable ending possible, in which the absence of discovery is the guarantee that riot continues—"we can now all do as we like."

The dark side of a lack of denouement in farce is apparent in those farces of Molière that leave the victim (George Dandin, Le Barbouillé) caught, cuckolded, and in a deadlock made more unbearable by his knowledge of the truth. There is madness at these endings as well, but it is not riotous. It is a feature of the comic victim's trap.

More than farce, the Old Comedy of Athens lies outside the main European literary traditions of comic form. It is probable that even learned comic poets like Ben Jonson, who acknowledged the greatness of Aristophanes, did not use him as a model.[24] All the rhetorical criticism of comedy, with its divisions into parts and analysis of stereotypes, was founded on the example of New and Roman Comedy. Despite the strangeness, it is interesting to see that the problematics of ending as we have outlined them above are not irrelevant to Aristophanes. The first thing one notices is the obvious importance of the notion of riot to the study of the closing movement in Old Comedy. Not only does one comedy end in a violent riot *(The Clouds)*, but the victory processions and wedding songs of *The Acharnians, The Birds, Lysistrata,* and *Peace* all enact and refer to ecstatic celebration and implicitly or directly invite the audience to take part.[25]

Riot is an acceptable ending in Old Comedy as it is not in the major kinds of comedy afterwards, because exuberance and unrestrained vitality are appropriate to the unambiguous victories that Aristophanes' endings celebrate. The drinking, dancing, and sexual activity, even the pogrom of *The Clouds,* the selfishness of Dikaeopolis enjoying his victory, as well as the shared happiness of the Spartans and Athenians in *Lysistrata*—all these prodigious and moving fantasies of release are unique compromises between wildness and social forms. The libidinousness and the *schadenfreude* are strongly stated, but they are not out of control, as riot threatens to be in later comedy. On the contrary, they are part of the socially acceptable and divinely sanctioned festive excitement that includes insult, beatings, and drunkenness, as well as marriage and reconciliation. In the last dance-songs of *Lysistrata* the Spartan and Athenian choruses make us aware of the difference between secular riot, which is a threat to happy endings, and divinely sanctioned riot, which is the comic chorus's expression of gratitude for victory. Among other deities, the Athenians call on Dionysus to witness their revelry, their leaping steps, while the

Spartans conjure up images of young girls leaping ecstatically like Bacchantes. This is riot in praise of the gods; its loss of control is possession by the divine force. As such it is a movement of completion, a high point as opposed to the farcical function of riot, which is to cause absurd giddiness. Therefore Old Comedy does not have a modulating action to tame the energies that create the comic display because those very energies, having defeated the enemies of wit and the good life, are present without reservation at the end.

There is, then, no need of discovery to turn the action in the direction of ending. On the contrary, the characteristic discovery in Old Comedy is at the beginning, when the witty initiator of the action challenges the given order. Dikaeopolis decides to opt for a personal peace, Pisthetaerus and Euelpides give up Athens for the Bird Kingdom, and Lysistrata decides to recruit her sisters against the war. The whole play that follows is a testing of that discovery through contest and trial, until the enemies of the witty project are defeated. Thus the shape of these comedies emphasizes both opening and close. The opening astounds with the originality of its fantasy, while the close crowns that fantasy with success.

Deadlock is not emphasized, partly because there is no intrigue to speak of, but mainly because the Old Comedy's vitality is one-sided, giving little freedom to the enemies of wit. Yet even here the peculiar partnership of deadlock and riot is a major catalyst of comic solution. In *Lysistrata* the breakdown of the men and their will to war is preceded by the excruciating temptation scene in which Myrrhina tantalizes her desperate husband, Cinesias, with elaborate preparations for love and then disappears. There is no more graphic image of deadlock in comedy than the body of poor Cinesias stranded in erotic expectation. Riot follows, not as real movement, but fantasy, as he imagines in a dialogue with the chorus, Myrrhina thrown up by a whirling hurricane and flung through the air to land miraculously on his member. The Shakespearean riot of *A Midsummer Night's Dream* and *The Comedy of Errors* is the result of error and has to be transformed: Cinesias's dream of violent god-given sex is a hyperbolic foretaste of the real ecstasies of the end. It need not be transformed or modulated, only translated by peace into blissful reality.[26]

Satirical comedy peopled by gulls and tricksters, by monstrous humors and caricatures of vices, is another kind of comedy that tends to move towards an explosive climax through the accumulation of preposterous and outrageous incident. It moves awkwardly towards resolution, and even off the stage it does not find ending easy. Satires are essentially lists of complaint, tables of examples showing how bad things are. Juvenal notes and angrily describes each separate monster as it comes into view in the crowded Roman thoroughfare. He is not telling a story and has no plot.[27] The shape of the satirical list is climactic. Things get more and more monstrous and if an end is imagined, it is the apocalyptic triumph of monstrosity: "Lo! thy dread Empire, CHAOS! is restor'd."

Parallels in drama to Pope's dark vision at the end of *The Dunciad* are rare, perhaps because the social bias of theatrical convention has always demanded some judgment and some vindication of traditional values. Shakespeare's *Troilus and Cressida* is an unusual example—a satirical play that comes close to ending on a note of total chaos. There the confusion of ignoble battle and unheroic death mocked by the barking, cynical observer, Thersites, is too close to the end to be modulated into something more flattering to accepted pieties. No heroic deus ex machina intervenes to assert order, and the last word is left to a pimp. But such extremism is not characteristic of ending in dramatic satire. The chaotic riot of human ugliness is no way to end a comedy; conventionally the confusion may be interrupted by the entry of a figure standing for stern justice or by the acknowledgment of a power outside the play capable of purging the evils dramatized in it. Such figures are the king's representative in *Tartuffe,* the Queen in *Every Man out of his Humour,* and the real Government Inspector in Gogol's play.

In formal terms, satire, like farce, often does without prolonged denouement. Instead it deploys the forces of riot and deadlock as close to the end as possible and relies on the saving interruption. Denouement, because of its involvement with modulated stages of discovery and recognition, is out of place in satire, where the victims' ability to bear discovery is minimal. Discovery explodes them. As for the knaves, they are either victorious or defeated, with no need for a process of unraveling to lead from the former to the latter.

In satire as in farce, there is a strong element of riot that feeds an action and moves with accelerating speed and through an accumulation of damning examples toward a situation that combines explosion and judgment. But that riot is mental rather than physical. As a principle of forward movement in satirical drama, riot is the wild fantasy that fires the mind of both the knave and his victim. The central figures of dramatic satire are comic overreachers. They want everything. Mammon wants to turn the world to gold, Volpone wants to play ever more daring tricks on his gulls, Tartuffe wants to possess all Orgon has, including his wife, and even Gogol's miserable Mayor has a detailed vision of what decorations he will wear and how the best horses will be held for him when he begins his new life in Petersburg. These dreams of pleasure and power have the energy of riot about them because they would defy exhaustion. As fake carnivals they would suspend reality indefinitely, putting in its place no principle but that of their own gratification. But their weakness is that they are fakes. The riotous energy of both victim and trickster in satire is based on lies. Its flamboyant fraudulence is fragile. That is where satiric riot is caught and punished. Its fragility is at the heart of its monstrousness. Volpone's flamboyant tricks depend absurdly upon the loyalty of Mosca, Mammon's dream is spun out of a shabby bluff, and Tartuffe's monstrousness shrinks to nothing in the eye of the all-powerful king.[28]

The combination of riot and deadlock is an especially salient feature of ending in satire. In earlier examples we have seen how these qualities are often simultaneously present, as in the climactic sequences of comedies like the forest scenes of *A Midsummer Night's Dream,* where riot is the external expression of a state of deadlock. In satire deadlock is as much a feature of character and its relationships as is riot. At the end it is perhaps of more weight than either riot or resolution. Although we have discussed the satiric character's fantasies and projects in terms of would-be riot, the moral bias that directs the satirist in creating such a character leads him to stress the deadlock implicit in the character's fixations. Both victims and knaves in satire are conventionally "humours" or caricatures, extreme stylizations of some weakness or vice. Despite their flamboyant dreams, the satiric art that has created them has made them unchangeable monomaniacs, obsessed men, and this is even true of those knaves, like Volpone, whose flexibility and improvising wit are a camouflage of their humor. If riot expresses the unreal dreams of such characters, deadlock expresses the judgment always implied by the moral tone of satire, but most apparent at the end. Imprisonment, chaining, the giving of true names (wittol, fool, knave), and the spectacle of frozen gesture *(The Government Inspector)*[29] are signs of judgment and discovery, but also of the knot that ties a fool to his folly and a villain to his villainy for good.

This deadlock may not apply to all. Khlyestakov is still moving at the end of *The Government Inspector,* "bowling along now, with all his bells a-jingle, laughing his blasted head off!"[30] Face survives all the reversals at the end of *The Alchemist.* For these witty or lucky knaves the riot continues, and their escape introduces an element of genial laughter into the battlefield of exploded humors and frozen caricatures. Although the rigorous, morally appropriate end is discovery and judgment, which freeze the humors, such punishment is hard for comedy to digest without turning nasty. Thus even the central humor has a way of surviving. Volpone survives his punishment through the mask of the actor appealing to the audience to whom he has given laughter. Our clapping is a different kind of judgment from that executed on the stage.

At its subtlest dramatic satire circumvents the harshness of its judgments. In some of Molière's plays the humor who initially blocks true love and is himself deadlocked in obsession survives by the mediation of an elaborate ceremony in which the sane adapt themselves to the mad, for the good of both. In *Le Bourgeois gentilhomme* and *Le Malade imaginaire* the ceremonies that involve "comédiens" or professional actors within the fiction are a genially comic, but also ironic means of getting away from the need to destroy a humor to achieve the happy ending. Even if they are tricks played by actors, and perhaps because they are, these ceremonies reintroduce riot not as the harmful, greedy fantasy of the central humor but as a game, played by all, whose purpose is to allow madness breathing room. Béralde calls it carnival.[31] As carnival, it is a therapeutic riot, but unlike carnival it is, for the humor, endless. He will never have to wake up.

The types of comedy I have considered so far have not stressed change or recognition. Satire and farce are constructed on the hypothesis that characters act with a rigorous consistency that may be interrupted or reversed like an act of religious conversion. Old Comedy emphasizes reversal, victory and defeat rather than transformation. In most of these cases there seems to be little room for an elaborate modulating action to mediate between the struggle and turbulence of the middle and the conventions of ending. Instead riot and deadlock press to the very close and often only the quick interruption of an outsider makes it possible to achieve an acceptable ending. The closeness of riot and deadlock to the final curtain makes a rarity of recognition if that has anything to do with a character's growth into understanding. It also makes it harder for the audience to contemplate the niceties of recognition because the hectic comic rhythm suggests that other things are more fun. At the end of *The Alchemist* we are asked to enjoy the tricks and delight in the continuing ignorance of all London. The delightful point about Face is that his witty role is able to survive in spite of his exposure by Lovewit. The master's discovery of what has been going on in the house does not bring the trick to an end nor does it hinder his participation in the profits of the enterprise. On the contrary, he is sucked into the whirling trickery and plays his part as well as any of the knaves. Recognition here becomes an auxiliary to riot and those who lack it are despatched into the streets of London locked into their folly.

It is Shakespeare's comedies with their romantic bias and stress on recognition that set out an alternative way of linking epitasis and catastrophe, desis and lysis, deadlock, riot and discovery. To understand this alternative structurally it is worthwhile looking briefly at the practice of Roman comedy, which was more than any other form the model of the Renaissance comic playwrights. The plays of Terence and Plautus display many of the features already discussed under the headings of farce and satire, but they stress one that farce and satire neglect and that is the formal sequence of discovery.[32] It has been argued that such a sequence is rarely found in satire and farce. These kinds of comedy have no story to speak of and the characters at the end have nothing to tell each other. They are either screaming or silent; nothing new can be learned about them. But Roman comedy has romance-like stories in its background, stories of shipwreck, misfortunes of war, stolen babies, and hidden love affairs. The sequences of discovery in those comedies are a way of leading the action towards equilibrium by adding the story's missing part, which assigns to each character his proper name, status, and past. This sequence, which sometimes resembles the stages of a Euclidean proof, is one means by which the gap between deadlock and happy ending is bridged. The analytical, logical, and prosaic tone of the discoverer, the *persona ad catastrophem machinata,* is often in sharp contrast with the high emotions of the deadlocked central characters. His sometimes quite elaborate series of questions introduces an earthy proof of the astonishing roundabout of comic chance that brings children back to their parents and makes outrageous love affairs turn out to be respectably matched marriages. Although the sequence of discovery is the supremely conventional path to the happy end in Roman comedy and though its artificiality is proverbial, the fact that it is a sequence and not a lightning reversal makes a subtle exploitation of feeling also possible. Characters can be observed growing into awareness. They come to wrong conclusions and are led to the right ones. They are stuck in impasses until the real identities dawn on them. Thus in Plautus's *Captives* the father's questions of the slave lead him through trial and error to the discovery that he has tortured and enslaved his own son. Then when the prisoner is brought out of the quarries in chains the sequence is repeated as the son surfaces with difficulty out of his pain and ignorance.

This is the kind of discovery Shakespeare found in the Roman tradition. In that tradition there is not only the conscious art and trickery of denouement but the dramatization of an awakening that reorders the past by isolating the fortunate links between distant accident (a casual liaison) and present crisis (the young man loves the daughter of that liaison). Terence's *Phormio* is not that far away from *The Tempest*.[33]

In the most humane and complex comedies, like Shakespeare's, the device of recognition and the whole sequence of denouement take on a new importance. The dramatists tended to make fun of the arbitrary element in comic endings. Edmund in *King Lear* jokes about the absurd timeliness of Edgar's entrance: "Pat! he comes, like the catastrophe of the old comedy."

Molière in his dramatic discussion of attitudes to comedy in *La Critique de l'École des femmes*[34] has his characters reach an impasse. They have no suitable denouement to end their discussion, which they want Molière to turn into a play. Neither marriage nor discovery is appropriate in this case. They are trying to think of something when the lackey enters: "*Galopin:* Madame, on a servi sur table." They jump at the God-given solution. What better denouement is there than the interruption of a servant calling everyone to dine?

Dorante replies, "Ah! voilà justement ce qu'il faut pour le dénouement que nous cherchions, et l'on ne peut trouver de plus naturel" (sc. 7).

Both Shakespeare and Molière are joking about the lucky chance that unties comic knots, but these examples obviously do not tell the whole story. The action of resolution in the most subtle comedies exploits the well-tried tools of convention, but in ways that make us seek meaning in what we might have taken for a trick. The basis of the weightier treatment of resolution lies in the way certain great comedies deal with the past in their concluding actions. The notion that the comic plot enacts a return is a familiar one. As I noted earlier, it is stated succinctly by Eugenius in the *Essay of Dramatic Poesy* in his explanation of classical descriptions of plot structure. In Eugenius's account, denouement—things "settling again on their first foundations"—is made possible by the removal of those "obstacles which hinder the design" and creates assent by its "resemblance to truth and nature." In comedy this kind of circle may describe the action of simpler rather than complex plays. For instance, it well describes the return to false respectability at the end of *An Italian Straw Hat*. There equilibrium is reached but the whole point is the absence of change. There is no change, because as is appropriate to farce, there is no recognition.

The most humane comedies do account for change and rely on recognition (reevaluation of the past) to help bring it about. Although they do not ignore the characteristic comic logic that stresses the consistency of foolish and ridiculous behavior, or in terms of our earlier analysis the persistence of deadlock and riot, they find ways of breaking out into a qualitatively different experience, or if not, at least of reconsidering and reevaluating the experience of their characters' past.

It is in Shakespeare's essentially romantic comedy that we find at its clearest the modulation of riot and deadlock by recognition into change. It is in such comedy that the greatest weight and room is given to the device of discovery, until in *The Tempest* it is present from beginning to end, no longer a device but the *ethos* of the plot. Not only does Shakespearean comedy experiment with the extended discovery, it also links epitasis and solution, but separates both from the end by as much as an act so that in *A Midsummer Night's Dream* and *The Merchant of Venice,* the significance of the untying can be ironically contemplated and its magical or moral meaning weighed. In the group of plays that end in trials *(All's Well That Ends Well, Measure for Measure, Cymbeline)* an elaborate scene of judgment coincides with denouement. Here in a judicial context the mistakes and sins that tied the play's knot are exposed layer by layer in a drama whose subject is recognition, even if its protagonist does not achieve it. Even in an early play like *The Comedy of Errors* in which the riot of farce pushes close to the end there are two sequences of recapitulation that respectively act out chaos and set out the meaningful pattern that frames it. Linking all these examples is the presence of the past, the remote as well as the immediate past, in the comedy's concluding action. In itself this is not surprising. Recapitulation is a clear way of framing an action. But the importance of recapitulation in Shakespeare's endings is anything but merely formal. It has to do with the tendency of his comedy to enact an optimistic and moral plot in which the review of the past in scenes of discovery reveals finally a meaningful and sometimes a religious pattern. This is the way Shakespeare's romantic comedy escapes the essentially linear thrust of that comedy that gives more weight to riot, deadlock, and repetition than to recognition and change. Instead of the freeze, the explosion, victory, and defeat, Shakespeare's comedies bring about a return, sometimes more perfect, sometimes less, sometimes understood by the characters, sometimes fully understood only by the audience, but always an image of beneficent, morally revealing change. This change is the opposite of the riotous alteration that often occupies the middle action of the comedies and in which the characters lose themselves in error. It transforms instabilities of feeling without doing violence to consistency of character. It is paradoxically both change and return, and its symbol is the circle image of perfection and of the interdependence of beginning and end.

The significance of return in the Shakespearean comic plot may be illustrated by reference to contrasting ideas of change and return in Ovid and in Spenser. The Elizabethan imagining of the destructive and obliterating power of alteration is well known to us from many sources, notably Shakespeare's sonnets and the *Mutabilitie Cantos* of *The Faerie Queene.* The erring stars, disloyalty in politics, treachery in love, and schism and heresy in religion—all these failings in nature are ascribed to the maleficent force of change that can be opposed only by the tough resolution of a personal integrity or by the appeal to a source of stability outside nature: ". . . that same time when no more *Change* shall be."[35] Yet both in Spenser's *Mutabilitie Cantos* and in Ovid's *Metamorphoses* the unsettling flow of perpetual change is in the very circularity of its motion seen to establish a kind of stability. This is the stability of circular movement in which growth and decline, progression and return, merge into each other as earth melts into water, water refines into air, air becomes fire, and fire thickens back into air:

> The earth resolving leysurely dooth melt to water sheere.
> The water fyned turnes to aire. The aire eeke purged cleere
> From grossnesse, spyreth up aloft, and there becometh fyre.
> From thence in order contrary they backe ageine retyre.
> Fyre thickening passeth into Aire, and Ayer wexing grosse,
> Returnes to water; Water eeke congealing into drosse,
> Becommeth earth. No kind of thing keepes ay his shape and hew.
> For nature loving ever chaunge repayres one shape anew
> Upon another.[36]

In Ovid this circle speaks of the inexhaustible copiousness of life that renews itself through the casting off and donning of shapes. It appears to be morally neutral, an obvious and cogent image of an observable natural fact given a comforting significance. In Spenser, Nature's answer to the claim of Mutabilitie that the universe and all things in it are subject to her, retains the ideas of the circle and the perpetual return but introduces the notion of change with a purpose, that of achieving perfection. Nature admits that: ". . . all things stedfastness doe hate;" but change is according to her neither simply a sign of the copiousness of creation nor an admission of the rule of disorder. The circle is the sign of perfection and the meaning of change is in the fated return to the true *perfected* self:

> . . . yet being rightly wayd
> They are not changed from their first estate;
> But by their change their being doe dilate;
> And turning to themselues at length againe,
> Doe worke their owne perfection so by fate:[37]

There is in these lines a Christian affirmation of the individuality of the self, the created thing in nature that finally resists change because God created it unique. The pagan's endless chain of metamorphoses dissolves character in the colorful variety of new shapes issuing out of nature's store. Spenser's Nature ties change to the surviving oneness of character and to God's planting of perfectibility in his created things.

The Spenserian and Ovidian cycles of change provide us with analogues for a similar circular figure found in the plots of Shakespeare's comedies. The Shakespearean comic plot often draws its characters through a circle of bewildering changes and errors, which brings them back to themselves when they have worked their own perfection.[38] This circularity of "in my end is my beginning" may seem to be a banal enough formal feature of plots satisfying the minimal requirements of a pleasingly optimistic tidiness.[39] But it is more than that. It is the figure that distinguishes the tone and tendency of Shakespeare's comedies from those of most other great comic playwrights. It is the reason why his endings may often be said to "crown all" and why they often engage us on the ground of belief for which the classical examples of comic ending show little precedent.

2

How Comedies End

To have considered the tensions between the complicating factors of a comic action and the way they are or are not resolved is not yet to have discussed the actual devices that traditionally end comedies. There is a surprisingly limited catalogue of major devices, all of which have the function of closing off the action within the play and of modulating the movement from the world of the play, with its conflicts and collisions, to the daylight world of the audience. The simplest of these devices are extrinsic to the play and the body of the plot. They are epilogues and requests for applause, conventional but often used with subtle effect to remind us of the continuing hold the finished action has on our imagination. The more complex devices are strictly part of the action as it has developed and betray and even intensify its confusions and characteristic rhythms while displaying the artifice that will bring them to resolution. Thus the untying action of *Twelfth Night* is built up of a series of false recognitions and perplexing confrontations that serve opposite purposes; they increase the confusion but bring true recognition closer. Closing sequences in comedy look back to the energy of the epitasis while unfolding the pattern that quells this energy and molds it into acceptable social forms. Their formality and artfulness is often the expression of a conflict between control, more obvious as the play reaches its end—and the recalcitrant energies that are the source of much comic action.

Lorenzo Da Ponte, Mozart's librettist, considering the problems of ending comic opera in the late eighteenth century, confronts the question with a witty sense of the challenge that the finale poses to composer, librettist, and performers alike:

This *finale,* which must remain intimately connected with the opera as a whole, is nevertheless a sort of little comedy or operetta all by itself, and requires a new plot and an unusually high pitch of interest.

33

The finale, chiefly, must glow with the genius of the conductor, the power of the voices, the grandest dramatic effects. Recitative is banned from the *finale:* everybody sings; and every form of singing must be available—the *adagio,* the *allegro,* the *andante,* the intimate, the harmonious and then—noise, noise, noise: for the *finale* almost always closes in an uproar; which, in musical jargon, is called the *chiusa,* or rather the *stretta,* . . . The finale must, through a dogma of the theatre, produce on the stage every singer of the cast, be there three hundred of them, and whether by ones, by twos, by threes or by sixes, tens or sixties.[1]

For Da Ponte the finale is above all an exhibition of art. Everyone must be allowed to show off his powers; singers, players, conductor, designer of effects, and composer. It must therefore be quite a long sequence, displaying all the different kinds of singing and the various kinds of voices. Because of its length it will have a unity of its own, or its own plot, like the final set of tricks in *The Marriage of Figaro,* which contrives to bring the whole cast on stage. Thus a ball, a party, or a wedding are ideal occasions for finales. With everyone on stage, everyone singing, and the orchestra showing off its tricks, it is not surprising that the whole thing should end with "noise, noise, noise"— the great *stretta* in which words surrender to joyful sound.

It is clear why the *stretta* is so desirable at the end of comic opera. The joyful, noisy climax is comic riot tamed by music. Something that without music would be close to confusion or absurdity is through music given a shape. It is the sound of release, the closest perhaps the modern stage can get to the licensed riot of Aristophanes' endings— and yet it is pure convention. That is the power of the comic ending; its way of embodying, arousing, and satisfying strong and perhaps opposing feelings through conventions that are blatantly artificial and yet expressive.

First, in our catalogue of devices are conventions of ending that are strictly outside the closing action because they tell the audience explicitly that the play is over. *Please Clap.*

Because it is a musical imitation of riot, Da Ponte's *stretta* is the opera's way of turning to the audience for applause. The happy noise on the stage is the signal for an equivalent outburst from the audience. Turning to the spectator is the simplest and most ancient way of announcing the end. It is possible because the presence of the audience is acknowledged in all comedies through the physical intervention of laughter, while in some this presence is continually stressed through direct address. *"Plaudite,"* says the actor in the Roman comedy, even if, in the play, he is the victim of the comic trick (like Plautus's Pyrgopolynices in *The Braggart Soldier*).

Epilogue. Applause, like laughter, is vital to comedy. Its absence at the end of tragedy may be a sign of deep feeling; its absence at the end of a comedy is an unambiguous sign of disapproval. Without it, the play may be said not to have achieved its "end," which is to please. Applause puts the seal of communal approval on the art of actor and poet, which without it is stranded in isolation on the stage. Epilogues are an elaboration of the plain Roman request for applause. But on the Elizabethan stage they have a more subtle status. There epilogues often occupy the interesting half-light between the illusion of the stage and the clarity of day. In the comic practice of Shakespeare and Jonson the epilogue is usually spoken by the trickster, whose wit has spun out the comic action (Face, Volpone, Prospero, Rosalind, Puck), and it is therefore both an apology and a claim for his art, which is also that of the comic poet. Like the Roman actor's inviting his audience to the feast,[2] the Elizabethan epilogue may extend the illusion of the play and by asking us to approve of a character's art (Face), make us accomplices in it. Through epilogue applause becomes a consciously purposeful act: we moderate the severity of Volpone's sentence, we send Prospero a wind, and unpleasantly, we clap to "cure" the pathologically noise-hating Morose. Epilogues are then a way of delaying ending, like encores. They extend the illusion beyond the stage and invite the spectator's conscious participation in the comic world at the moment of its disappearance.

Play. The actor's confrontation with the spectator through the epilogue is a simpler version of a similar confrontation that occurs as a device of ending within the play itself. Epilogues, as we have seen, expose the play's art, apologize for it, and make claims for it. They do this before an audience that knows all the play's secrets and may have been changed by that knowledge. Plays-within-the-play and scenes of conscious theater work similarly when they occur—as they often do at the end of comedies. First, they parade art; they expose the bare bones out of which the imaginative miracle was wrought. The penultimate moment of *Bartholomew Fair* is devoted to a gross, obscene puppet play, a travesty of the story of Hero and Leander. It is the lowest form of theater, like Bottom's play, but on its level, it works. The noisy puppets have an appreciative audience and reduce to silence Busy, the Puritan enemy of the stage. Such displays of specifically theatrical artifice are appropriate to the endings of comedy because they forestall, by including it in the body of the play, the objection that comedy is a lot of nonsense and signifies nothing. Yet the exposed art that in one play reveals the absurd foundations of comedy, in another makes

large and serious claims for itself. Theater is an image of transformation, capable of effecting sublime as well as base changes. So the
final scenes of *The Tempest* and *The Winter's Tale* are scenes of theatrical discovery in which a curtain is parted to reveal a tableau that
comes to life and enters a changed reality. Prospero and Paulina are
presenters of these scenes, stage managers who have arranged for a
miracle to happen. In such scenes the technical set-up of theatrical
discovery (the curtain, the space behind it, the music) becomes indistinguishable from the idea of discovery as a process of spiritual change.
Miranda and Hermione come out of their "discovery space" into their
stage audience, which has earned this recognition scene. But play-
within-play endings may stress the opposite. If the epilogue turns to an
audience that knows all, the play on the stage may turn to a stage
audience of "know-it-alls" who know less than they think. This happens in *A Midsummer Night's Dream,* where our ironic distance from
the happy lovers is measured by our perception of what they fail to see
in *Pyramus and Thisbe.*

Recognition, achieved or missed, tends to be the major topic of the
play-within-the-play convention at the end of comedy. The illusion of
the theater presents to the characters a final mirror image of themselves or of their wishes just before they and everything else on the
stage vanish. Sometimes the mirror releases the image, it becomes real
and takes part in the final reunion. Sometimes the illusion draws its
audience into itself, as in the carnival ceremonies of *Le Malade imaginaire* and *Le Bourgeois gentilhomme.* In the former case, wish
becomes reality through art and the recognitions it has fostered. In the
latter reality conforms to an eccentric wish through the good offices of
a comic art that dispenses with recognition.

In the above instances the image of theater at the end of comedy
engages comic art at its opposite poles. At the one end there is absurd
artifice and noise (puppets); at the other, there is sublime artifice and
transformation (Hermione). Common to all is the focus on the base
material, the trickery out of which dramatic illusion generally, but
comic illusion specifically, is created.

Trial. Plays-within-the-play create an opportunity for the gathering of
all the characters in one place around a presentation that retells a
version of their story in some way while displaying the dramatist's art.
A trial is also a gathering of this kind and it is, like the "theater" ending,
preoccupied with recognition and show. Trials at the end of comedies
are always chaotic and disturbed ceremonies in which the confusions
and deadlocks that reigned in the middle action are replayed in quick
time and in a compressed space until a surprising interruption either

forces judgment or makes it unnecessary. Whether they are formal trials before a court or a supreme authority *(Volpone, Measure for Measure, All's Well That Ends Well)* or informal scenes of petition before a prince *(The Comedy of Errors)*, their attempt at a rational reconstruction of the past inevitably loses itself in a maze of contradiction. Thus they imitate riot while attempting to bring about a just conclusion. In this way they enact the difficulty of discovery in situations where it is in fact only the drop of a mask away.

Trials as ending devices in comedy are theatrical above all when they are based on an illusory crime. Bertram did not deflower the Florentine virgin; Angelo did not execute Claudio or sleep with Isabella. Like the device of theater such trials bring about recognition through the exploitation of illusion before an ignorant audience. The judicial forms and procedures, like the adducing of evidence, cross-examination, speeches of accusation and defense, are essentially fake because neither the judges nor the victims have full knowledge. Such trials are then elaborate preparations for the discoveries that will give them meaning. It is that discovery which enables justice to be done, although it does not always bring about a moral recognition *(All's Well That Ends Well)*.

Unmasking.   Trial is a process leading up to discovery; unmasking is the act itself. It is the drastic final gesture of disguise plots, a potentially powerful coup de théâtre, whose exact placing in the final sequence of a comedy determines the nature of that sequence.

The most climactic unmasking is the one longest delayed and closest to the final curtain. This is the discovery that makes a fool of everybody including the audience *(Epicoene)*. After it nothing more can be said. It is the crowning gesture of a successful trick and recasts the whole play in its light. Its opposite is the discovery that initiates the final scene *(As You Like It)*, making the ending sequence of the play a considered elaboration of its consequences. This is a fully controlled, rational act foreseen by the audience, expected and enjoyed for what it is. It is the source of words rather than their defeat.

Unmasking in romantic comedy is never as radical a change as that of *Epicoene*. The revelation of the girl in boy's dress always has something ambiguous about it that holds her to her rejected disguise and hints at a certain continuity. This is the natural result of the structural tension between male and female in the leading role of such plays as *As You Like It* and *Twelfth Night*. Its clearest expression is Viola's remaining in her page's suit. Physical transformation would be a crude climax for his ending, which is therefore marked by the ambiguity, the unfinished quality, of Viola's imperceptible alteration.

Few unmaskings at the end of comedy are as unpressured as Rosalind's. In satires and farces it is likely to be violent, often the defeat of a plan, close to the end, and productive of few words (Volpone's "You hear me brief"). Because it is a gesture of climax, unmasking may be violent, even in a play where the masker is victorious. In *Measure for Measure* the Duke does not reveal himself but is unmasked by Lucio in an act of physical and verbal aggression. If violent unmasking is climactic, unforced revelation may be an anticlimax, as is the case with Overdo's discovery in *Bartholomew Fair*. He reveals himself to discover that his act changes nothing. Unlike Rosalind he is not in control of the play's final action and his unmasking therefore reveals his weakness as a judge.

Unmasking is the theater's simplest image of recognition and most radical image of change. This is usually a change from illusion to reality. So in those rare comedies in which the final movement goes in the opposite direction and allows the illusion to continue there will be a new masking. This is what happens in *Le Bourgeois gentilhomme* and *Le Malade imaginaire*. In these plays an ironic solution is sealed by the device of a new mask.

Repetition.   Repetition as a central structural feature of satire and farce is creative of endings that underplay recognition. It is an expression in such plays of the consistency of the humor that may survive ending. The gag of the runaway train that accompanies Buster Keaton in *The General* is still with him in the final frame of the film. But repetition may also be a tool of recognition. One of its functions is to bring the plot to the point of exhaustion, ignoring the past; the other is to encourage ironic contemplation through contrast with what has gone before. The first kind is a rhythmic principle by which similar situations are almost identical, the difference being perhaps an increase in violence or in speed (*The Comedy of Errors*). Yet within the farcical framework, repetition may also be a way of intensifying an unchanging situation. Thus in *George Dandin* the husband is cheated and blamed a number of times in a similar way. The last time is simply the most outrageous, most explicit, and most shameful. Beyond it there is nothing, only death:

> s'aller, jeter dans l'eau, la tête la première.
>
> (3.8)

In Jonson's satire the structural skeleton of the play is the repeated encounter of knave and gull. Under the pressures of accident, coincidence, and time, these encounters follow each other more quickly.

They grow more violent as verbal aggression turns physical and the humors become ripe for expulsion. The last scenes of *The Alchemist* pass all the victims in review; each receives his parting blow and is dispatched into the cold world. This is the same structure as that of the opening, and it sets out delightfully the absence of recognition. The humors have been disappointed but they go into the world with their obsessions unchanged. Repetition here is not a principle of exhaustion but one of endless extension. Dapper is still in London somewhere, believing his "Aunt of Faery" is going to make him a millionaire.

The second function of repetition is closely related to the possibilities of recognition at the comic ending. It is technically different from repetition in farce and satire in that it is not a matter of a chain of similar situations but rather of a major crisis of the play's middle action being replayed in a distorted way at its end. This makes it a powerful tool of irony because the spectator who grasps its significance is superior to the characters who do not. Because it focuses attention on the past (the incident of the rings in *The Merchant of Venice*), this sort of repetition is not climactic. Instead it asks us to reflect on the similarities and differences between the middle epitasis situation of deadlock and danger and its mirror in the moments before the resolution. Our acceptance of that resolution, then, is informed by a renewed consciousness of the crisis out of which it grew. This is our recognition, if not the characters'. Only in Shakespeare's romances does the moral pattern of repetition impress itself on spokesmen of recognition in the play. That is what Gonzalo understands by the discovery of Ferdinand and Miranda in *The Tempest*. He observes a miraculous pattern of losing and finding in which everybody takes part. For Gonzalo the awareness of the pattern's repetition is a sign of miracle. For us the ironic option remains as we consider the variety of human types included in the pattern.

The difference between this use of repetition and that in Shakespeare's romantic comedies is that the latter isolates a specific situation that bears on the ending ironically, while the romances proper stress a general pattern whose comprehensiveness is not seriously challenged at the end.

Sequence and Tableau. The final scenes in comedy tend to create a stage picture that is a succinct expression of the play's ethos. Because of the presence of convention this picture is prone to symbolic interpretation. Thus we interpret the dance at the end of romantic comedy as a sign of resolved erotic energy and the binding of knaves in satire as a way of condemning them to be themselves forever. Because of the formality of the arrangement of characters at endings we become especially aware of any break in symmetry. Division into couples may be offset by the odd man out (Antonio in *The Merchant of Venice*) and the simple fact of an exit may draw unusual attention (Malvolio). Given the formality and the narrowing range of possibilities for action as the end approaches, the sequence leading up to the curtain may become a concentrated restatement of all that ending has to deal with.

Usually it is a matter of bringing all the characters on stage to participate in the conclusion. More rarely the sequence is one in which the stage gradually empties. The full stage is the spectacle we associate with celebration, the empty stage with defeat, and we find it therefore in satire or in unusually serious comedies.

The most formal sequence is one in which the reappearance of the major characters and the restatement of the main themes is ordered by some social convention like that of the court of law. In these cases the order imposed by the convention is continually threatened and indeed upset by the explosiveness of the revelation to which it is advancing. This tension between conventional or visual symmetry and order and the unruly heritage of the consequences of the middle action is an important factor in many ending sequences that then contrive to continue the struggle while formally announcing its end.

In romantic comedies the final tableau is traditionally one of couples arranged for a dance or for a procession. In the simplest case *(As You Like It)* the stability of the final arrangement is undisturbed by confusions surviving from the past. Thus the sequence leading up to the exit is one in which an odd and deadlocked arrangement of lovers becomes even. The unsymmetrical tableau is made symmetrical by the formal entry and revelation of Rosalind. The neat division of the stage into couples finds expression in language through the repeated valedictory epigrams in which the fate and future of each separate couple is summed up. Only Jaques disturbs the balance. He is the one figure on the stage who does not fit in. A far more complicated sequence is the one that leads to the exit procession in *Twelfth Night*. Here there is no ceremonial formal structure at all; the occasion for the end is simply the first meeting in the play of Olivia and Orsino. The sequence is composed of a series of "unplanned" entrances. There is no center; no one is in control. Instead, the stage gradually fills up as each character bearing his fragment of experience enters the scene. This fragmentation emphasizing division and struggle rather than unity is not easily overcome by the revelation of the twins. Here again, the turbulence of error is brought right into the formal confrontation of ending. In the final tableau the emphasis is again not on balance alone but also on things left unfinished, such as Malvolio's unresolved anger and Viola's undisplayed womanhood.

The harmonious dance and procession of ending in romantic comedies celebrates the group of lovers even though the final sequence may have encouraged us to look ironically at what constitutes it. In satire the group of gulls is condemned and expelled. The final sequences of such plays therefore move towards the spectacle of arrested action or towards an empty space peopled only by a few survivors.

The tableau of arrest is the succinct stage picture of what satire insists upon telling us: that a fool is married to or possessed by his folly. It is prepared for by sequences that prolong the violent energy which fuels the caricature's career until the doom of discovery. Unlike what happens in romantic comedy, this turbulence does not militate against the conclusiveness of satirical ending. In satire the only way to cut off riot is by revelation, and the juxtaposition of the two expresses the drastic nature of the sickness and the radical nature of the remedy. In *The Government Inspector* the final sequence begins with the entry of the Postmaster, reading the letter that affixes the appropriate scornful names to all (crook, half wit, pig, dog). But the caricatures are not trapped yet. The revelation produces riot, in the Mayor's outburst and attack on the audience, and in the general assault on the miserable Bobchinsky and Dobchinsky. The real Inspector's arrival is announced when the riot is at its height, and the curtain goes down on a tableau of immobility superimposed on hysteria.[3]

The silent stage of Gogol's ending is at the opposite comic pole to the joyful noise of Da Ponte's *stretta*. In the same way the empty stage of some comedies is the opposite of the crowded finale of celebration. The final sequences of *The Alchemist* are devoted to a gradual emptying of the stage, which is at first full of curious neighbors, then busy with final trickeries until, the last victims disposed of, Face and Lovewit are left alone to face the audience. Emptiness here is a visual image of trickery, the nothing out of which so much activity was created, and a symbol of the victory of the knavish imagination over folly. In this it is close to the emptiness of the stage hinted at in Puck's epilogue. In the latter's apology for art the bare stage is said to have yielded "but a dream." No one was cheated, except an audience that presumably collaborated in the trick. In *The Alchemist* the empty stage is the sign of a profitable cheat, and Face's invitation to us to clap makes us into his collaborators.

Although it seems a contradiction, the empty stage at the end of *The Alchemist* is a festive emptiness, brimming with the vitality of the successful trick, and potentially full of the feasting audience. There is nothing festive about the bare stage at the end of *Le Misanthrope*. In Molière's play there is also a progression from a full stage (the letter incident) through a gradual series of pointed exits, to the final spectacle of Alceste at the extreme and logical point of his career walking off in search of his solitary salvation. The bareness and silence at this curtain is the tableau that conveys the full imprint of Alceste's nature, unrelieved in this case by the usual arrangement of happy couples around the odd man out. Molière, defying convention, which would have made Alceste's exit an expulsion, instead makes the stage at the end an image of the bare ascetic fantasy of his unexhausted humor.

Comic endings are surprisingly concerned with the past. Because of the "happily ever after" formula, we think of these endings as imagining a bright future, but then a study of comedies shows how a review, replay, or narration of past events is a feature of ending in very different kinds of plays. Why is this so? A comparison with tragic ending shows that speeches concerned with the past at the ends of tragedies tend to be formal and confined to a specific event. That is what the great messenger's description of catastrophe does in classical or neoclassical tragedy. Choric lament, or the hero's final assertion of himself may also unfold through a comparison between present downfall and past glory. But the high tension and pathos of a tragedy's final scene usually leave little room for a recounting of the events that brought it about. If not provided for by the messenger convention, this recounting is fragmented, smuggled in unobtrusively so as not to disturb the direct confrontation with the spectacle of suffering and death.

Comic endings, on the other hand, confront us with nothing so much as art or artfulness, and even when they approach sublimity they do this by making a metaphysical design appear out of the artful pattern of the comic plot. The need to recapitulate before the end is the poet's need to display the cleverness of his contrivance by numbering its parts shortly before its dissolution. Recapitulation in farces, as well as in the subtlest comedies, makes us aware of a logic in the comic plot that may either please as an elaboration of absurdities or attract belief as a pattern of something cogent and whole. The reappearance of all the characters to be awarded their fates may be a sign of celebration or satirical defeat. More generally their reappearance together or in sequence is another reminder of how obtrusive pattern is in comedy and how ending is so often achieved by a shuffling around of what was already displayed at the beginning. The systematic review of characters and themes, though it often involves riot and confusion, gives comic endings a formal authority other than the social authority of weddings, dances, and processions. It is the authority of something fully worked out, a riddle answered, an apparent impossibility proved possible—in short, a conscious superimposition of a formal pattern on material that may until the very last moment whirl with turbulence.

In the following three chapters I consider characteristic patterns of ending in groups of comedies by Jonson, Molière, and Shakespeare. A study of both the formal and thematic problems raised by the endings of individual comedies is likely to yield a fresh understanding of specific plays and contribute to our knowledge of how comedy works. That is why I have chosen to consider plays by three dramatists who represent the essence of dramatic comedy in the sixteenth and seventeenth centuries. The work of these dramatists is a flowering of comic traditions that go back as far as Aristophanes; yet their comedies are still performed and interpreted on the modern stage. Thus a study of their endings may reasonably be expected to reveal new or confirm old perceptions about the structure of comedy in general.

3

Perplexing the Catastrophe: Endings in Jonson's Comedy

The rewarding competition between riotous comic energy and the intellectual lucidity of an artistic pattern is one of the factors that gives Jonson's major comedies their vibrancy. Though he was a declared moralist,[1] his successful comedies enact their plots of victorious or defeated trickery with mainly ironic reference to public morality. It is rarely the judges, lawyers, or officers at the end of his plays who bring about discovery; they are either part of the cheat (the mock lawyers in *Epicoene*), victims of the bluff *(The Alchemist),* mere observers of the struggle that leads to unmasking *(Volpone),* or subjected to exposure themselves *(Bartholomew Fair).*[2] What is more, the audience is twice called upon in epilogues to approve of the knavish performance (*Volpone* and *The Alchemist*) in terms that specifically subvert legal practice.[3] Conclusion in three of these plays, whether it punishes or rewards the tricksters and wits, is primarily the abrupt completion of an elaborate and consistent internal pattern. It is the successful or unsuccessful outcome of stratagems that, whether known from the start, as in *Volpone,* or revealed only at the end, as in *Epicoene,* are seen to organize the whole play. Only in *Bartholomew Fair* is trickery not an organizing principle. It is also the only play in the group that takes discovery seriously as an act of reevaluation and change.

Criticism of the structure of Jonson's great comedies has followed two main conceptions of what that structure is. The traditional conception is mostly indebted to Dryden's praise, in the *Essay of Dramatic Poesy,*[4] of the unity of plot in *Epicoene*. Dryden sees the play as an action leading to one end: "the action of the play is entirely one; the end or aim of which is the settling Morose's estate on Dauphine" (p. 83). Dryden notices both the rhythmic structural principle of a more and more crowded and riotous action, "the business of it rises in every act" (p. 88), and the spatial elaboration of a design that is laid out like a garden with an eye to variety to relieve the order—the "by-walks, or under-plots, as diversions to the main design, lest it should grow tedious" (p. 88).

Eliot was the first modern critic to point to an alternative way of looking at the structure of Jonson's comedies. He saw the "immense dramatic constructive skill"[5] but found this to be "not so much skill in plot as skill in doing without a plot." By plot Eliot meant the elaborate complications of romantic comedy and the intrigues and counterintrigues of Restoration comedies. What he found in Jonson was an "action" rather than a plot; in other words, a simple principle of movement given significance by what he calls "unity of inspiration." Following Eliot's hint, later critics like Ray L Heffner, Jr., and Ian Donaldson[6] have elucidated the unifying ideas, symbols, and conceits that in their view give the plays their characteristic structure.

A student of Jonson's endings happily can have it both ways. Taking a hint from Jonson himself he will be interested in ending as the completion of a stage sequence, a final twist of plot that displays the manipulating skill of the inventive dramatist, incidentally akin to the manipulating skill of his cheaters:

> Stay, and see his last *Act,* his *Catastrophe,* how hee will perplexe that, or spring some fresh cheat, to entertaine the *Spectators,* with a convenient delight, till some unexpected, and new encounter breake out to rectifie all, and make good the *Conclusion.* (Chorus, between acts 4 and 5, *The Magnetic Lady,* 27–31)

But the student of comic endings will not merely chart "the processe, and events of things, as the *Poet* presents them" (Chorus 12–13). The devices of ending that Jonson uses are blunt but less conventional than they seem. Essentially they are devices of discovery and unmasking strongly ironic in effect. They "make good the *Conclusion*" in a way that transcends the witty logic of a cunning plot and may be said to cap the action by summing up in a few pointed gestures or in a clearly defined sequence the central tensions that give each action its characteristic comic energy.

There is only a minimal untying action in these plays. Denouement is a feature of romantic plots that the bias of Jonson's comedy rejected. The major action of *Volpone, The Alchemist,* and *Epicoene* is a tying action in which the riotous plot-making energies of wits are pitted against the follies and obsessions of their victims in relationships that for all their turbulence are going nowhere. Morose's desperate cry in *Epicoene,* "O, the varietie and changes of my torment!" (5.4), is applicable to the less sadistic embraces that lock together Volpone and his victims and Face and his gulls. These are essentially situations that could go on for as long as the greed and the blindness of the victims are matched by the greed and cunning of the knaves. Especially in *Volpone* and *The Alchemist* Jonson has created self-sufficient, self-consistent worlds of chicanery that outside intervention cannot penetrate. This is true, though less subtly, of *Epicoene,* where the impenetrable secret is Dauphine's master trick. The clearest figure of this perfect bluff is the house in *The Alchemist* that is discovered to be empty by the pack of gulls and officers who burst into it in the final scene. This emptiness is another way of putting the failure of unmasking and the defeat of discovery. The end of this play contradicts Jonson's moralizing about imposture in the *Discoveries:*

> *Imposture* is a specious thing; yet never worse, then when it faines to be best, and to none discover'd sooner, then the simplest. For *Truth* and *Goodnesse* are plaine, and open; but *Imposture* is ever asham'd of the light. (236–239)

In Jonson's comedies, even in *Volpone,* imposture parades itself and seeks the light of a world in which discovery from outside is impossible because truth and goodness are not believed or even given a hearing in court. In the satire discovery is not "a miracle," as the gullible and discredited judges call it in a series of speeches that parody recognition (5.12.95–99). The unmasking comes from within. The knot is undone as a conscious if desperate act: "I must be resolute" (5.12.84) by the knave who tied it. Recognition is primarily that forced on Mosca by his master, who "uncases" and makes the servant call him by his rightful name, "Patron." Volpone, by discovering himself ("I am VOLPONE and this is my knave," 5.12.89–90), takes the functions of the judges away from them and attests to the integrity of the comic pattern that destroys the cheat by deploying the very same energies that built it up. Volpone, a figure of riot as a masker, a weaver of lurid fantasies and a baiter of folly, is ultimately trapped by transformation itself:

> Nay, wee so insist in imitating others, as wee cannot (when it is necessary) returne to our selves: . . . (*Discoveries,* 1095–96)

This is, as Jonson noted in the same passage of the *Discoveries,* what makes life like a play (1,093). This emphasis on imitation as a trap is very different from the world-stage analogy we find in such writers as Shakespeare and Erasmus. For them the playing of many parts is an image of transitoriness. The actors play, as Erasmus says, "until the manager waves them off the stage."[7] For Jonson the actor becomes what he plays. Mimicry becomes habit and is its own judgment. The idea accounts both for the impudent masquerade at the center of *Volpone* and the defeat of masking by itself.

The endings of the plays of imposture come from within. The trickster defeats himself, the clever knave absorbs his master's return and saves the hoax, the gentleman wit proves his superiority over dupes, fellow wits, and the audience by suddenly revealing the true sex of Epicoene. At the center of these plays is a lie that attracts riches and creates an elaborate and turbulent comic action. At their end is a gesture of discovery (unmasking, breaking into the house). The turbulence of the action, its speed, noise, disguisings, its displays of baseness and folly are the surface features of essentially static confrontations that the endings accentuate and do not transform. The pattern of trickery remains constant in these plays to their last moments; in *The Alchemist* it even survives the end.

Discovery, even when moral, as in *Volpone,* is not separate from this pattern. Rather, it is the last "cheat" in a series—Volpone cheats Mosca. This kind of discovery seals the world of the trickster plays in its own consistency, which is doubly sealed as the audience is given the role of connivers with wits *(The Alchemist),* noisemakers, and torturers *(Epicoene)* and amused judges of the knave *(Volpone).*

Only in *Bartholomew Fair,* among Jonson's successful comedies, does the ending make us take discovery seriously. In the other plays the riotous action of noise, disguise, and trickery repeated in situation after situation confirms the immobility at the center. The ironic unmasking of Epicoene and the self-destructive uncasing of Volpone may be coups de théâtre but they do not move the plays out of the confines of the trick. Overdo's unmasking is not a surprise. He has been contemplating it since the early part of the play. Discovery of enormity is his purpose and theme. But the anarchic earthiness of the carnival, turning all things upside down, also turns his aim of thunderous exposure into a display of his own weakness. Overdo discovers that he is part of the chaos (flesh and blood) and not its judge. Thus he is converted, not like Lovewit before him into part of a secret, closed world of trickery, but into an acceptance of his part in a common, vulnerable humanity. The play opens outward at its end and includes wits and fools at the banquet table.

In the *Discoveries* Jonson notes briefly the dependence of a puppet play on dim light to create belief:

A *Puppet-play* must be shadow'd, and seene in the darke: For draw the Curtaine, *Et sordet gesticulatio.* (*Discoveries,* 240–41)

In *Bartholomew Fair* the light is shone on the puppet. He reveals himself in his "nakedness" to the ranting Puritan. But this discovery does not discredit the puppet; rather it transforms Busy from a fierce critic into a spectator. That gesture sums up the special quality of *Bartholomew Fair*'s ending—it reveals all, but not cruelly. Despite its baseness it is a genuine gesture of release and an invitation to change.

Volpone demonstrates most clearly the tension between the morally conceived idea of what ending should be in a satire and the amoral energies that fuel the plot. Embodying these energies, Volpone, despite the elaborate art with which he is created, is close in some ways to a puppet we have already considered, the wily and malicious Mr. Punch. Like Punch he is a caricature of human nature and his appeal to us is founded on the violent egocentric and amoral energy that such a caricature can display. Like the puppet, Volpone is engaged in a battle of wits against a series of victims who are no match for him. But unlike Punch, Volpone is finally held accountable for his "past misdeeds and frolic and fun," condemned by the reverent Avocati, and then partially reprieved by the poet with the connivance of the audience. As we can see from his dedicatory *Epistle,* Jonson was aware of the oddness of his ending, which, he points out, he could easily have changed. He persisted with the savage ending "to put the snaffle in their mouths that crie out, we neuer punish vice in our **enterludes**"—in other words, to prove that comedy can be moral.

Jonson's problem in ending his play is the problem of the satirist complicated by the nature of his protagonist. The material of satire is human degradation and folly, and the task of a satirist is to make this material as real as possible by giving every shamefulness its name, and labeling every last foul stench. If the assumption of satirical writing is that men are hopelessly corrupt, the satirical plot can have no positive end. If it envisages an end it may be the deadlock of a Gulliver in human society, or the victory of Universal Darkness in the *Dunciad*. A movement out ot the morass can only be initiated by some extraneous figure like the Queen, whose presence clears the air at the end of *Every Man out of his Humour.*

In *Volpone* Jonson certainly creates a corrupt and unnatural human scene scrupulously detailed, both in the graphic commentary of Volpone and Mosca and in the self-revealing words and gestures of their victims. The dramatic climax of the play's depiction of Venetian baseness may be placed in the first court scene (4.5.6) in which a monstrous battery of perjured rhetoric (Voltore), false evidence (Lady Would-be), and ghoulish trickery (the "sick" Volpone wheeled in for display) is aimed at the innocent victims, Celia and Bonario. There is in the play no more obvious expression of the triumph of evil than the exit into custody of the innocents and the return of Volpone, laden with apologies, to his lair. It is a moment made for thunder, for a sign of retribution, but as yet there is none. Instead, the epilogue to the court scene is Mosca's as he whispers to each victim the mocking praise or assurances that ensure his continued control over them. Lady Would-be's final words, "You shall sway me" (4.6.101) sum up the whole scene. This is the monstrousness that the ensuing action of the play has to fashion into an acceptable end.[8] The general outlines of such an end are clear enough in advance; fool and knave will be punished and innocence vindicated. But the crucial questions are how will this come about, and how differently will fool and knave be treated?

The fifth act of *Volpone* is a recapitulation of the play in double time, reenacting its major situations, unburdened with extraneous matter, but pregnant with the burden of ending.[9] The violent activity of the preceding four acts has, as the result of strenuous effort by the knaves, returned them safely to their starting point. Volpone's disguise remains unpenetrated, the victims remain benighted, the cheating may begin again. Thus the Volpone who opens the act, a little upset but soon encouraged by wine, is the tarnished reflection of the mock heroic figure who first greeted his pile of gold with a hymn. Yet his plan is a more daring one than any concocted in the past. He accepts the challenge of Mosca's:

> Here, we must rest; this is our master-peece:
> We cannot thinke, to goe beyond this.
>
> (5.2.13–14)

Then, by feigning death, he creates a trick that is structurally like the opening situations but qualitatively different. Again the procession of possessed victims files into the lair, to encounter Mosca and be watched from behind the curtain, but whereas before, the confrontation with each victim was oblique and Mosca's aggression restrained by the need to keep the victims interested, now the clash is direct. It is the end of the road for the legacy-hunters:

> Go home, and die, and stinke.
>
> (5.3.74)

This is the last we see of the play's most characteristic situation, and its exhaustion as a possibility leaves Volpone facing Mosca in the narrowing ring of the plot. The next repeated situation is Volpone's exit from his lair in the shape of the Commendatore. In his first excursion in disguise, as the Mountebank, Volpone's delight in his artistry permeated the shabby rhetoric of his quackery. His disguise then was a trap for idiots such as Sir Pol and, perhaps, for beauties such as Celia. For Volpone it offered an active and showy contrast to his passive role of bedridden impotent. In act 5 his disguise is called by Mosca "the Foxe-trap," and the opportunity it affords Volpone for abusive or ironic rhetoric at the expense of the legacy-hunters is less important than our understanding that the knave's new clothes signal a drastic reduction of Volpone's opportunities for action. Disguise in the re-capitulating action, then, does just the opposite of what it does in the rest of the play. Instead of freeing, it imprisons the masker and ensures that the consequent unmasking will be a forced move, the last in the play. The unmasking of Volpone is indeed the climactic moment of this act, and in its self-destructive desperation is to be contrasted with the masterful, if grotesque, flourish of his unmasking before Celia. There the throwing off of bedclothes risked discovery for the prize of beauty; here the unmasking in the courtroom ensures discovery for the doubt-ful compensations of revenge:

> I am VOLPONE, and this is my knaue;
> This, his own knaue; this auarices foole;
> This, a *Chimoera* of wittal, foole, and knaue; . . .
>
> (5.12.89–91)

The earlier unmasking paradoxically revealed Volpone in yet another fantastic role, that of a gallant lover. This one reduces him to his name, and the whole group to their proper place in the catalogue of men and beasts.[10]

The replaying in act 5 of situations we have watched before is Jon-son's way of preparing us for the inevitable end. Repetition itself is the structural backbone of comedy based on fixed character types, and given the premises of satire, the cheat could go on forever. The efficient cause of Volpone's downfall is, of course, his own insatiable hunger for more aggression. In this way he is possessed as much as his victims are, and like them, must be purged or dispossessed. Like Mar-lowe's Barabas he must repeat his trickery until he tricks himself into destruction. But Jonson does not follow the model of the linear series rising to its single climax. By creating a false end at act 4 with the victory of evil, and then restarting the plot, Jonson creates a self-contained final act in which each major figure displays again his vir-tuosity or folly in such a way as to arrest all further possibilities.

Like acrobats in a circus finale, Volpone and Mosca go to greater lengths than before, take greater risks as the space of the plot narrows, until all that is left is the confrontation and unmasking before the court. By the nature of its repetitions this act underlines the inevitability of the catastrophe, while continuing to entertain us with the spectacle of trickery. The moral logic of repetition can therefore replace the weak claim of the Avocatori to represent retribution. True retribution is not in the sentence of the compromised court, but lies in our perception of the difference between Volpone's unmasking before Celia and his un-casing of the Fox at the end.

One more uncasing has to be mentioned—the epilogue. At the end of the play Volpone comes forward, half in his role, half out of it, to appeal to another kind of court for another kind of sentence.[11] He wants applause from the audience in gratitude for the pleasure (if only *schadenfreude*) afforded by his knavery:

> He, yet, doth hope there is no suffring due,
> For any fact, which he hath done 'gainst you; . . .
>
> (3–4)

As in *The Alchemist* the knave comedian makes a subversive appeal to the proper audience on the basis of the amoral pleasure he has given them. Volpone cunningly puts the alternatives: censure or clapping jovially. Jonson knew, despite his *Epistle*,[12] that his knave figure was in terms of theater invincible and that like Mr. Punch, his fun, frolic, and misdeeds would gain the applause of any audience that knew how to laugh.

The Alchemist has one of the most patterned plots in English comedy. Jonson's genius in constructing it has often been pointed out, notably by Coleridge, but pattern is not an end in itself, and in this play, its tangible presence points to the conflict that gives the work much of its irrepressible vibrancy.

Like *The Comedy of Errors,* it is a play that declares at the beginning that at a certain fixed point it is going to end. In Shakespeare's play this point is sunset, by which time the old father will either find his ransom or have to die. The time limit is reinforced by similar arrangements in the parallel plots, thus creating the rhythm of racing time by which the characters' movements are paced. In Jonson's comedy the *terminus ad quem* is much vaguer—the return of Lovewit from the country. It depends not on something tangible, like sunset, but on a change in the death count of the plague. It therefore could happen any time and works as an interruption, the common ending of comedies that enact riot. The witty quality of this *terminus ad quem*—and it is essential to the suspense and vibrant energy of the tricks—is that it can be ignored by the tricksters. For them, caught in the whirling, improvising action of their confidence trick, there is no approaching end:

Face: O, feare not him [Lovewit]. While there dyes one, a weeke,
     O' the plague, hee's safe, from thinking toward *London.*
                                                          (1.1.182–83)

And yet ending, the exposure of the trick, is a recurring possibility
from the very opening, and one can describe the plot as an increasingly
complicated struggle between the wit, which always seeks new opportunities of trickery, and its enemies, which would expose it and foil it.
The uniqueness of the play's ending is that the trick remains undis-
covered, and the unmasking of Face and his return to Jeremy the butler
become a way of successfully exploiting and continuing the illusion
around which the play is built.

The play's elaborate plot structure is the dramatic image of the balance between an almost perfect confidence trick and the forces that
would explode it. Its elaborateness is actually a complication of a
simple dramatic figure—the confrontation between knaves and victims
in a limited space (the Blackfriars house). The pattern becomes involved as the confrontations crowd upon each other, as the space in
the house becomes peopled with victims, and as the plotters have to
improvise solutions to chance interventions that threaten to destroy
their profitable structure. This plot pattern is a kind of contest between
the poet and his artist-protagonists (Face and Subtle). If they manage
to preserve its logic, they win the prize of wit. The dramatist keeps
throwing obstacles in their way to test them. At the end the ironic logic
of the pattern is victorious along with the wit, who alone was able to
overcome all the obstacles.[13]

The pattern of the confidence trick involves the imposition of its
order on essentially wild material. Its aim is to prolong the profitable
enterprise as far as possible. But in this it is in conflict with whatever in
the play is pushing toward a definite end. The most drastic end is
discovery, and it is always a possibility, but it never happens. The most
common "ends" are those desired by the victims, who wish to see the
results of their investment in the art of the "holy man." The witty
knaves attempt to preserve the pattern of their device (the plot), an
increasingly more demanding effort, by putting off all endings except
those that they contrive to rid them of gulls who can be led by the nose
no longer.

The very opening of the play is a loud and rambunctious display of
the violence (noise and physical assault) that the common plot must
defeat if its pattern is to work and foil discovery. The knaves seem
likely to destroy their successful trick before the play has got under-
way, and the spectator may well think he is witnessing the culminating
scene of a satire as he hears the list of damning names:

Subtle: Cheater.
Face: Bawd.
Subtle: Cow-herd.
Face: Coniurer.
Subtle: Cut-purse.
Face: Witch.   (1.1.106–8)

This is in fact a scene of discovery, perhaps *the* scene of discovery in a play in which the failure of discovery is a structural principle. At the end of the play similar words are used as the angry gulls burst into the empty house. But nothing and no one are discovered there. This movement, from vulgar exposure in the opening scene to the bland surface of Jeremy's "innocence" and Lovewit's pretense of ignorance, is an ironic movement, celebrating successful trickery and subverting the moral significance of recognition. Lovewit discovers Jeremy's trick, only to be drawn into it.[14]

The near discovery of the opening scene, only foiled by Doll's righteous anger, is replaced by a new pact to "labour, kindly, in the commune worke" (1.1.156). This is the signal for the pattern of encounters to begin. These encounters, apart from displaying in great detail the banal and mock-heroic fantasies of an array of dupes, draw much of their tension from an inner battle between the ends envisaged by the victims and the knaves' devices to foil them. The simplest victims, like Dapper, are so malleable that their illusion can have no end, and it is fitting that this character and his peer Drugger should come and go throughout the play as leitmotivs of passivity. They can only exemplify and not disturb the pattern imposed by the wits. This is made clear at the height of the closing frenzy, when Dapper's intrusion from the privy is absorbed without bringing about discovery.

The real challenge to the pattern of wit, and the best example of the play's tension between discovery (ending) and continuing illusion is Mammon, the heroic grotesque and his tough, unlaughing companion, Surly.

As a heroic humor, Mammon displays the characteristic contradictions of the type. He is a figure of riot, possessed of a fantasy that is inexhaustible—"I see no end of his labours," says Subtle, (1.4.25)—but his career in the play, because of his fantastic pretensions, must also reach some end. His illusion, unlike Dapper's, would provoke action in the real world. He awaits practical results ("This is the day" 2.1.6), Mammon is therefore a figure on whom the conflicting forces of riot and discovery concentrate, and the absorption of this threat by the pattern of wit is its greatest victory. Mammon's "end" is to "turn the age to gold," and the knaves' "end" is to coin Mammon into profit; the victory of the knaves enables the plot to go on. The strategy by which this victory is achieved shows well how pattern and wildness coexist at a climactic moment in the play.

Mammon's end, or rather the defeat of his fantasy, is a mock discovery, a foreshadowing of the futile discovery at the end when the cheated rabble rush into the house to find it empty and its wealth irretrievable. Its symbol is explosion. This is already hinted at in the printed *Argument* to the play, which describes the varied activities of the cozeners:

Till it [the stone], and they, and all in **fume** are gone.

The smoky fume is the equivalent of the emptiness that the successful cheat leaves behind it, an emptiness that provokes anger and thoughts of revenge but denies discovery. Mammon's defeat is also a violent emptying of the overblown fantastic humor, leaving ashes where there were golden thoughts. It is engineered in a way characteristic of the comic pattern of the play by the incorporation into the pattern of a seeming accident. Doll's appearance at the door on the cue "common" (2.2.210) is the beginning of an elaborate sequence that leads to the explosion by way of a grotesque wooing and the eruption of Doll's esoteric babbling. The wildness of the noisy nonsense from Puritan tracts, the "accident" of Doll's appearance, the explosion of the *"Retorts, Receivers, Pellicanes, Bolt-heads"* (4.5.61), the fainting of Subtle, all this is in reality controlled action. Unlike the hysteria of the chase in *A Midsummer Night's Dream*, it does not enact deadlock. The opposite is true. Its sets out the possibility of the cheat going on for as long as the cheaters wish. It is a mock ending, just as it is a mock discovery. The bits of metal brought by Mammon for transformation into gold are sold to the Puritans, and so the cheat seems to be eternal and self-sustaining, a successful order imposed on the greed and gullibility of all the random clients thrown up by London one day during the plague.

Mammon's discovery is a cruel parody because it does the opposite of what discovery traditionally achieves. It prolongs his illusion. The parody is made more extreme by the victim's use of religious language:

O, my voluptuous mind! I am iustly punish'd.

(4.5. 74)

and

> Good father,
> It was my sinne. Forgiue it.
>
> (4.5. 77–78)

His exit is engineered like the bait that trapped him. An "accidental" knock at the door is interpreted by Face as the arrival of the furious "brother" of the raving woman:

> . . . Auoid his sight,
> For hee's as furious, as his sister is mad.
>
> (4.5. 67–68)

Mammon's exit in 4.5. is then the epitome of the cheater's art. Coincidence, accident, and improvisation have been ordered into a purposeful pattern by "teeming wit." The aim of this pattern is to prevent discovery, and the incorporation of fake discovery is therefore its master stroke.

Mammon's discovery is his defeat, because he cannot break out of the illusion so carefully built around him by the wits. But surly's unmasking, which follows it (4.6), is the most serious attempt at discovery since the opening scene. Surly is not a fantastic humor. He has no dream, and his gross sense of a base reality puts him at odds with the fantasies of the house from the beginning; his humor is suspicion:

> Faith, I haue a humor.
> I would not willingly be gull'd. Your *stone*
> Cannot transmute me.
>
> (2.1. 77–79)

He is the knaves' most dangerous enemy because he is an opponent of wit in his refusal to believe and yet can make use of the devices of wit in an attempt to destroy it. Apart from Lovewit he is the only outsider who disguises, but unlike the former, his disguise is a weapon of discovery rather than a sign of collaboration in the pattern of wit. Surly makes the one genuine gesture of discovery in the play. He unmasks, calls the thieves by their rightful names, and assaults Subtle physically:

> *Surly:* Will you, *Don* bawd and pick-purse? How now? Reele you?
> (4.6. 26)

His threat is doubly emphasized by his explicit understanding of the trick of explosion. He knows what the smoke of nothingness means in the strategy of the wits:

> And this Doctor,
> Your sooty, smoakie-bearded compeere, he
> Will close you so much gold, in a bolts-head,
> And, on a turne, conuay (i' the stead) another
> With *sublim'd Mercurie* that shall burst i' the heate,
> And flye out all *in fumo?* Then weeps MAMMON:
> Then swounes his worship.
>
> (4.6.40–45)

Here the comic pattern seems to be turning on its authors as one of its pawns rebels and calls the whole game in question. But discovery is impossible, given the self-contained nature of the plot and its center—the house—because no one outside the circle of fantasy can arrive to destroy it. Subtle's accusation is thus lost in the noise of the quarreling Kastril brought in by Face, the entry of the peripatetic Drugger, and the lucky "accident" of the return of Ananias the Puritan. All three, for different reasons, connected with their humors, turn on the unlucky Surly in his Spanish disguise, and he is dispatched in a cacophony of cursing and noise. The verbal explosion serves the same purpose as the havoc in the alchemist's laboratory that ended Mammon's career. It foils discovery, even when it is genuine, and it is founded on nothing.

The claustrophobic, rigidly delineated nature of the comic scene here makes discovery impossible and reinforces the pattern. The house is like a fortress: "how fares our campe?" asks Doll (3.3.33). In its treasury is booty that is brought by one victim and sold to others. In its rooms, privies, and "dungeons" various prisoners of fantasy are deployed. Its gates are besieged by others, who are clamoring for its panaceas. All this density is subject to the pattern created by the wits, who are able to change themselves to suit the particular fantasy of each client. Coincidence and accident create pressure, but the explosions, as we have seen, are put to use to prolong the pattern rather than destroy it. How, then, is it brought to a close?

The formal cause of ending is the one intervention that apparently cannot be drawn into the pattern, Lovewit's return from the country. The final act of the play is, however, a triumphal restatement of the witty pattern, bringing back all the victims, tempting them with discovery, and confronting them instead with the emptiness that is the image of their folly and defeat.

Lovewit's return is not the kind of interruption considered by Molière in his *Critique de l'École des femmes*. It is not the descent of an outside force that cuts off an action and imposes ending. This might have happened if Lovewit were a representative of justice come to expose and bind the knaves as well as the fools. But he is a wit, as his name declares, and his intervention becomes a collaboration with the pattern, so much so that its fantastic architecture remains undisturbed by the entry of reality. Only the people who control it change, as Doll and Subtle are expelled and replaced by the intruder.

Lovewit's return introduces a series of entrances that are unlike most of the previous entrances in the play. In the opening and middle action a character's appearance at the door was usually a sign of his entrapment in the net of the plot. Similarly his exit, like Mammon's, left his illusion unchanged. The series could, given luck, be endless. Lovewit's return coincides with the return of the principal victims as demanders of discovery. The repeated knocking on the door is apparently the herald of judgment. The language they use is the language of base truth, reminiscent of the opening quarrel:

> *Mammon:*   Rogues,
>   Coseners, impostors, bawds.
>
> > (5.3.9–10)

and:

> *Kastril:*   What rogues, bawds, slaves, you'll
>   open the dore, anone.
>
> > (5.3.33)

The pressure of the quick succession of angry clients at the door is a warning of the possible collapse of the structure of the cheat. Should the doors be forced the trick would be exposed. The danger of discovery comes also from inside. The securely closed logic of the pattern, symbolized by the impregnable fort, contains the gagged and incarcerated Dapper. His bleat for help—"Master Captayne, master Doctor" (5.3.63)—turns the pattern of the plot against itself at the most critical moment. The only way to save it is to turn the interrupting representative of reality (Lovewit) into a partner by teaching him the art of profitable improvisation that has defeated discovery so far. He'll get a widow by putting on a mask:

> 'Tis but your putting on a *Spanish* cloake,
> I have her within.
>
> > (5.3.87–88)

The action of these last scenes, like Da Ponte's finale, sets out once again but with the vibrancy of the race against discovery, all the ingredients of the play's witty pattern. Its rigorous logic, the logic of the trickster's art, has to be followed. So Dapper's interview with his

"Aunt of Faerie" is played out despite the crisis. The widow, there by chance, has to be married; the disguise of Hieronimo's cloak and hat has to be exploited.

There is a compulsive logic about all this that one would be wrong to attribute to Jonson's passion for lucid form. True, his classicizing art was in opposition to the untidiness of contemporary dramatists. But *The Alchemist*'s order, especially at its end, says something about the essence of that comedy and the meaning of the pattern imposed on the riotousness of its material.

The external activity throughout the play, and especially at the end, is wild. Noise abounds in the nonsensical tirades of Subtle and Doll. Entrances and exits point the accelerating rhythm, as do the frequent changes of mask by the tricksters. There is a baroque, verbal wildness in the fantasies of the heroic humors—Mammon and the Puritans. Yet this flurry of activity and mass of words are created out of a nothing— the emptiness of the bluff. The rigorous self-contained pattern of the plot is a way of keeping that nothing from being discovered. It is like a maze, cunningly laid out to prevent any approach to the center, and at the end, when the center is discovered, the angry horde finds nothing there:

> A few crack'd pots, and glasses, and a fornace,
> The seeling filled with *poesies* of the candle:
> And MADAME, with a *Dildo,* writ o'the walls.
>
> (5.5.40–42)

Thus discovery (the breaking down of the doors) is itself absorbed into the pattern of illusion. The reality of the house is as Lovewit has described it, an empty, shabby scene with a widow somehow placed in it. But the emptiness that faces the would-be discoverers and the representatives of the law is, for the surviving wits and the jovial audience, a copiousness that is the reward of trickery. The cellar is full of Mammon's metal, the chest is full of the profits of the business, and the widow is full of land and wealth that we are invited to share.

In many comedies the conscious display of pattern may be a sign of an essentially wishful optimism—that things may arrange themselves at the end. Its obviousness may leave room for ironic dissent. In this play the self-consistency of the pattern,[15] its lucid marshalling of characters in a cleverly exploited space, and its absorption of accident and interruption are a subversively rational way of justifying the amoral comic energy that Jonson invites us to approve and enjoy.

In the absence of the moral endings of discovery and judgment in the play, we, the only judges, are asked to do what Lovewit did—accept

Face's trickery as "decorum" and join in the profit.[16] If we laugh, clap, and approve as Face's "countrey"—i.e., his jury—the comic pattern tricks the world. It will never be faulted. It will have no end.

Epicoene is an unpleasant play and it has an appropriately unpleasant ending. The last sounds we hear are certainly not the joyful shout of Da Ponte's description of finale, but it is not quiet that sweetens Morose's ear as he departs the scene of his torture. The last word in the play is "silence," but Truewit's epilogue invites us to clap, to add our noise to the rowdy braying of trumpets, drums, and nonsense that has filled the theater at climactic moments in the plot. If we have followed the methodical baiting of Morose throughout the play our last act of approval before leaving the theater can only be our contribution to that assault.

Schadenfreude has always been an important factor in laughter, but its stressed appearance at the end of a comedy that is not explicitly satirical is rare. What is more, its presence here accompanies not the binding and exposure of a comic victim (the dupes in *Volpone*), but his *release* and therefore follows him offstage. The riotous noise of applause, the deadlock of Morose's unchanged humor, the ironic release of his divorce, and the freeing of his money clash disturbingly at this joyless end. However, if we concentrate on the act of unmasking we may see how it brings together the very different factors of ending.

Just as in the other plays of Jonson's that we are considering, the act of unmasking is a major, here the major, feature of ending. The example of *Volpone* showed how in satire unmasking was a clarifying gesture that combined self-assertion, defeat, and judgment. On the other hand the parallel act in *Bartholomew Fair* is an anticlimactic act of leveling and a failure of assertion and judgment. In both plays the culminating act of exposure draws its power from the way it imitates a series of similar acts already seen in the play. Face's exposure in *The Alchemist* is the most ironic because it is strategic, not a gesture of ending so much as a prolongation of illusion.

The unmasking of Epicoene is a highly successful coup de théâtre, a powerful and stable image of ending that brings to a sudden stop all the varied and involved actions of the play. Climactic like Volpone's unmasking but unforced, it is more like the announcement of the true Inspector General's arrival in Gogol's play than the other Jonsonian discoveries. It is the gesture that fixes its perspective on everything that has gone before by introducing a new discovery that is in retrospect totally in keeping with the play's opening situation and thematic development. The arrival of the real Inspector is deducible from the accidental acceptance of the fake. Gogol's logic is based on something outside his play—the reality of even a corrupt system of government. The logic of Epicoene's exposure as a boy has to do with some of the symbolic threads inside Jonson's plot. The discovery is their summation.

Although Epicoene's unmasking is most directly related to the plot against Morose, being the witty, surprising but inherently logical solution of Dauphine's dilemma at the beginning of the play, it is actually the culminating gesture of all the actions. All the different groups of characters present on the stage (and the audience offstage) are put in their places, duped as a result of this coup. The fool knights, Daw and La-Foole, are once more exposed as liars and empty braggarts; the pack of would-be fashionable women are shown to have revealed their feminine secrets to a boy; Dauphine's rival wits have to concede the prize of trickery to their cunning colleague, and finally, we in the audience have to admit that this was one trick we never thought of. Formally, then, it is a very satisfying end. It is the last piece in an elaborate puzzle, and its discovery and the fact that it makes the whole pattern logical are legitimate features of successful ending.

Yet the formal completeness clashes with a decided peculiarity in the emotional structure of the ending. Deliberately, indeed aggressively antiromantic, the play ends in a divorce (even *The Alchemist* has a marriage in it), in the sexual sterility of a boy coming out of girls' clothes—instead of the erotic possibilities of the opposite—and in the spectacle of the unchanged but defeated Morose. There is a sense of impasse here, a barrenness that is not subordinate to the jovial release of the misanthrope's money into Dauphine's spendthrift hands. The gesture of discovery, then, though a victory of wit, a joke to beat all jokes, is also a summation of far less genial thematic threads that are woven into all the parallel actions.

If the victory and enrichment of a wit is a festive ending, the exposure and defeat of dupes is satirical in its tenor. The combination is there in *The Alchemist,* where the emphasis is on the festiveness that we are invited to join. Here the emphasis is on exposure, a theme that the play's various actions have all rehearsed.

The empty, fashionable society that is the main context of the play cannot bear the exposure of the vanity or ugliness lying at its heart. This society is given its tone by women, and the most tangible image of its hidden secret is the reality of the face under paint. But the secret is also the reality of licentiousness under the pretense of respectability, folly masquerading as wit, and ignorance as learning. Apart from the baiting of Morose, the main conflict of the play is between the small group of wits and the pretenses they would expose. Each separate

device of theirs leads up to an act of exposure. Yet the wits are neither
moralists nor satirists; they themselves are part of this fashionable
society, and therefore their impulse to expose pretenders is inhibited
by society's rules and practices.

The opening debate between Truewit and Clermont (1.1) clarifies the
issue. The secret they are talking about is that of a lady's dressing
room, the door of which is usually kept shut to men and opened only to
the sexually ambiguous page. He sees the lady's face without paint,
and takes part in a little erotic game:

> shee kisses me with her oil'd face; and puts a perruke o' my head;
> and askes me an' I will weare her gowne; and I say, no; . . .
> (1.1.15–17)

Clermont hates the painting of the fashionable lady:

> A poxe of her autumnall face, her peec'd beautie: . . .
> (1.1.85)

However, Truewit, the most philosophical of the beaux, accepts the
game of surfaces and talks of makeup as a kind of holy rite:

> A lady should, indeed, studie her face, when wee thinke shee
> sleepes: nor, when the dores are shut, should men bee inquiring; all
> is sacred within, then.
> (1.1.115–17)

His description of a ridiculous incident in a dressing room sums up his
neutral[17] attitude to this kind of pretense. The story is of a lady, sur-
prised *en déshabille* by a "rude fellow." In her haste she puts her
peruke on backwards:

> *Truewit:*   And the vn-conscionable knaue held her in complement
> an houre, with that reuerst face, when I still look'd when
> shee should talke from the t'other side.
> *Clermont:* Why, thou should'st ha' releeu'd her.
> *Truewit:*   No faith, I let her alone, as wee'l let this argument. . . .
> (1.1.134–39)

Truewit is an ambiguous observer of this ridiculous spectacle. The
woman is cruelly exposed, bald and grotesquely wigged, the rude fellow keeps up a pretense of polite conversation, but Truewit, detached,
does not intervene.

> *Clermont:* Why, what should a man doe?
> *Truewit:*   Why, nothing: or that, which when 'tis done, is as idle.
> (1.1.32–34)

His acceptance of the social surface, despite his awareness of its vanity, alters the ground upon which the various actions of unmasking take place. Truewit's example suggests that if the cruel exposure of satire is out of bounds, unmasking is not a weapon but a game.

Still, Epicoene's discovery crowns two parallel plots of exposure, each one of which displays a specific kind of unmasking and its limitations in the given society of the play. The first is the wits' plot against Daw and La-Foole. The second is Truewit's plot against the ladies.

The plot against the fools seems to be a weak imitation of the similar mock duel between Aguecheeck and Viola in *Twelfth Night.* It is overlong and too obvious in its predictable sequence, like a joke whose end is seen from the beginning. But rather than compare it with the duel in *Twelfth Night,* one should see this device as analogous structurally to the "plays" that both Shakespeare and Jonson introduce into certain of their comedies at, or shortly before, their endings. Truewit's device is a piece of conscious theater. He sets the stage, the gallery, with a study at either end and provides for a chorus (his companions):

> here will I act such a *tragi-comœdy* betweene the *Guelphes,* and the *Ghibellines,* DAW and LA-FOOLE—which of 'hem comes out first, will I seize on: (you two shall be the *chorus* behind the arras, and whip out between the *acts,* and speake.)
>
> (4.5.30–34)

This "play," like the "plays" of *A Midsummer Night's Dream* and *Bartholomew Fair,* is a caricature, a reduction into much simplified lines of the enveloping action. Here it is a reduction of the very notion of "device" or "plot." Truewit's patent fooling of the two cowards, making them believe they are in danger, locking them up in two rooms, having them beaten and exposed before the ladies, is a concentration in a schematic sequence of what the plot elaborates piecemeal—the trapping, exposure, and punishment of folly. It is, however, the presence and reaction of the audience that gives the device its point. The exposure of fools is a simple task. It is complicated by the nature of those who observe such a spectacle. Here it is the ladies, themselves victims of appearance and fashion. The "play" exposes the unmanliness of the foolish knights graphically, and the ladies duly change their opinion of them. But through Truewit, Jonson finds this a false discovery, based not on truth but on "crude opinion."

> *Truewit:* Did not I tell thee, DAVPHINE? Why, all their actions are gouerned by crude opinion, without reason or cause; they know not why they doe any thing: but as they are in-

> form'd, beleeue, iudge, praise, condemne, loue, hate, and
> in æmulation one of another, doe all these things alike.
> Onely, they have a naturall inclination swayes 'hem gener-
> ally to the worst, when they are left to themselues. But,
> pursue it, now thou hast 'hem.
>
> (4.6.64–71)

Thus both the foolish actors and their false audience are exposed. The audience's recognition was of something that the "stage" really displayed (cowardice, stupidity), but they are blamed for their lack of consistency and judgment and for allowing themselves to be manipulated. They are an audience before whom exposure loses its worth, because they turn the spectacle into yet another one of the trivial entertainments that fill their day.

The last peripheral device of exposure is aimed at the group of women. Truewit (4.1) vows to make them all fall in love with Dauphine that day. This device is closely related to the "play" of the fools because Truewit arranges that Dauphine take credit for that coup. Creatures of "crude opinion" that they are, they transfer their affections to the new hero and crudely unmask their rivals to gain the new beau. Thus Centaur about Haughty:

> . . . she's aboue fiftie too, and pargets! See her in a fore-noone. Here
> comes MAVIS, a worse face then shee! you would not like this, by
> candle-light.
>
> (5.2.36–38)

The ladies, by slandering each other and by issuing lewd invitations to Dauphine, are showing what they really are, but their shame will never be made public. The wits will not expose the ladies because the social code does not allow it. At the end of the play it is Epicoene who is the repository of the ladies' secrets, but he will not blab because he will also shortly enter the life of courtship and fashion:

> And let it not trouble you that you haue discouer'd any mysteries to
> this yong gentleman. He is (a'most) of yeeres, & will make a good
> visitant within this twelue-month.
>
> (5.4.246–49)

Epicoene's unmasking is, unlike those discussed above, an unambiguous gesture. Unmasking in society was seen to be an ironic act. It did not define what was true, nor truly expose what was false. Epicoene's is a simpler gesture—a witty truth revealing itself and silencing all lies. Although it brings about the shameful expulsion of the braggart knights, it leaves the status of the ladies open. They are "mute" but the social talk and the "visiting" are shortly to begin again. It is thus an open ending, in spite of the silence it temporarily imposes.

Epicoene's gesture has been shown to be the summation of the peripheral actions; its relation to the career of Morose is more oblique. Morose, the noise-hating misanthrope, is a character totally outside the social world. He hates it. He wishes to shut it out. Because of his fearsome eccentricity, he is what he is. Masking is foreign to him, and unmasking therefore does not reverse him as it does the other dupes.[18]

Another conventional gesture of ending is used to enable Morose to leave the stage—the gesture of release. Dauphine makes a clear connection between his device of discovery and the act of release, as he whips the female attire off Epicoene:

> Then here is your release, sir; . . .
>
> (5.4.204)

Morose's exit is a release from the scene of torture, the "worst of all worst worsts! that hell could haue deuis'd!" But it is an ironic release into the privacy, silence, sterility, and death that are the consequences of his misanthropic humor—and when we clap in answer to Truewit's request we are still torturing him for his unchanged and surviving eccentricity.

The classical metaphors of plot structure, tying and untying, are put to work in a symbolic way in the baiting and defeat of Morose. They enable us to see Jonson's end as the sophistication of a traditional device, like the exploitation of unmasking in the other actions.

Morose is a classic anticomic figure of deadlock. The logic of his eccentricity—his hatred of company, of noise, of music, of festivity, leads necessarily to the impasse of silent isolation. In the play this state is symbolized by his house; at the end of the play, by his grave. He lives in a street that is a map of his nature:

> Why sir! hee hath chosen a street to lie in, so narrow at both ends, that it will receiue no coaches, nor carts, nor any of these common noises: . . .
>
> (1.1.167–69)

If this miracle of obstinate eccentricity changes at all, it can only be to a stone—a symbolic metamorphosis hinted at twice in the play (2.4.13; 3.7.23).[19] The irony is that he brings about change by his own initiative. Not content with attempting to change his immediate environment to suit his unnatural fantasy, he tries to go beyond it and assault the world. His project to find a silent wife and get an heir to disinherit

Dauphine is his downfall. Through it, like Volpone, he overreaches himself, venturing out of his protected isolation into the real world of marriage and children, and thus exposing the breach through which that world of turbulence and noise invades his fortress.

The character of deadlock thus becomes the victim of riot. Morose, "tied" to his obsession, tied to a talking wife, is like one of Captain Otter's bears, the object of a baiting, a "comœdy of affliction." Torture, Dauphine's "device of vexation," is here the assault of noise, words, trumpets, chaotic movement (3.7) on a victim who is tied to his stake (the house and his phobias). The victory of the assault, the height of frenzy, produces in Morose the most graphic state of extreme deadlock:

> Hee has . . . lock'd himselfe vp, i' the top o' the house, as high, as euer he can climbe from the noise. I peep'd in at a crany and saw him sitting ouer a crosse-beame o' the roofe, like him o' the sadlers horse in *Fleetstreet,* vp-right: and he will sleepe there.
>
> (4.1.21–26)

Morose has become metamorphosed into the device that expresses his impasse. Isolation, fixity, acute discomfort, and inhumanity make this vignette an emblem of his tied condition, a true mirror of both his obsession and of the progress of Dauphine's plot that manipulates this obsession for profit.

The problem of ending a "comœdy of affliction" is apparent in *Twelfth Night,* where the device against Malvolio gets out of hand and threatens to bring the anger of Olivia on the heads of the tricksters. In Shakespeare we sense a clash between the logic of "plot" and norms of human conduct, which are more forgiving of eccentricity and folly. In *Epicoene* the device is prolonged till the very end. The sequence of the "divorce," which is the enactment of untying—the release of Morose from the tortures of company—is used in a characteristic Jonsonian manner as a way of turning the screw some more. The mock denouement is itself a scene of torture, and the ritual of "untying" is accompanied by the noise of the mock lawyer's Latin and the protestations of the trapped Morose. The arranged entry of the angry cabal of women repeats the riotous invasion of the house in 3.6. Morose is thus in act 5 no nearer ending than he is at the beginning of his career:

> O, the varietie and changes of my torment!
>
> (5.4.9)

Epicoene's unmasking is therefore the only way of ending this affliction short of death, and it is connected with death because it comes when Morose has given away all his wealth in return for "the pleasure of dying in silence" (5.4.156).

The empty Morose is then confronted by the illusion (the boy) on which the elaborate structure of his torment has been built. It is a discovery for which there are no words. His silent exit is the logical outcome of his aggression against the world. He wanted to reduce it to silence and it has done it to him. Looked at from this point of view, the play enacts a battle for survival between a humor and a wit. Morose's victory would have imposed his unnatural image on the world around him and impoverished his nephew. Dauphine grants Morose his wish, ironically, "be as priuate as you will, sir," and releases the money.

Although the revelation of Dauphine's trick is a highly successful coup de théâtre, it makes for a less subtle ending than either the uncasing of the Fox or the discovery of the empty house. This is because the very perfection of Dauphine's cheat (he cheats us) reduces our awareness of the pattern of the play as it develops dramatically on the stage. It becomes a matter of hindsight. The audience's complicity is an essential element of the tension between judging and laughing in *Volpone* and *The Alchemist*. The knaves and wits are always implicitly performing before us and sharing their knowledge with us. This is why we have to be lenient towards them even if the law will not. Dauphine keeps his secret and this confirms our impression of the ungenial quality of the trickery in this play. There is much noise and turbulence but no positive energy at its center.

In *Volpone* and *The Alchemist* the comic interaction between the dangerous energies of wit and the fixed gullibilities of its victims is expressed through the intricate web of a lucid dramatic pattern. This pattern, the plot, is in both cases the construct of the wits, a product of their amoral art. Its consistency is enhanced by the action being mostly confined to one center and the victims being gradations and variations of closely linked categories of folly. In both plays the pattern remains constant to the end. In *Volpone* this constancy is the comic nemesis, the law by which Volpone outdoes himself and tricks himself into discovery. In *The Alchemist* the pattern of the plot incorporates the intruder from the outside world and thus remains undamaged, victorious over discovery. In these two plays Jonsonian lucidity works in opposite directions; in the satire the willful extension of the plot idea to its extreme causes it to collapse, while in the more genial play the artful manipulation of an outrageous idea makes it self-consistent and resistant to base reality.

In both plays the tension about ending has to do with a certain contradiction inherent in their given situations. In both the artful wits

dangle a tempting "end" in front of their possessed victims. That may
be the inheritance of Volpone's massive fortune or the transformation
of piles of junk into gold. Yet in each play, given the wit of the knaves
and the blindness of their victims, there is no good reason why the
cheat should not be endless. Jonson the moralist cannot allow this,
though Jonson the ironist does. But even in Volpone's case our applause in answer to the Fox's epilogue is evidence of a comic law that
values malicious fun at least as much as moral discovery.

Bartholomew Fair is a carnival play rather than a tricksters' play. Its
plot is not spun out of the teeming brains of a pair of wits and it does
not therefore have the consistency and unicentered quality of such
plots. Its unity has to do with a given place—Smithfield—and a certain
festive time, Saint Bartholomew's Day. But this place is multicentered,
made up of many booths, walks, and areas, and the time of the action
has no necessary termination. It is the idea of carnival that suggests the
rationale of ending in this play, and the character through whom we
perceive it is Adam Overdo.

The festivity of carnival, of which the fair is a specific expression, is
a limited and socially acceptable form of excess. Conventionally in
classical and in Christian cultures it takes place on a specific day or
number of days. On those days the normal rules of behavior that gov-
ern society are suspended and replaced not by utter chaos and anarchy
but by an alternative set of practices that allow freer expression to the
animal and instinctual aspects of civilized man.[20] Such practices are the
election of mock kings, the reversal of roles between master and servant, mock battles between virtue and pleasure, maskings that encourage free sexual activity, and of course overeating, overdrinking,
parodies, and play-acting. Excess of this kind may be said to exhaust
itself, just as drunkenness eventually gives way to sleep. But the in-
stitution of carnival, which frees its celebrants from so many necessities, is itself subject to the all-powerful necessity of time. At a fixed
hour the holiday must come to an end.

In his description of the Roman carnival of 1788 Goethe notes the
way that the frenzy of the final celebration surrenders to the approach
of midnight and the ascetic regime of Ash Wednesday:

No one can move from the spot where he is standing or sitting; the
heat of so many human beings and so many lights, the smoke from so
many candles as they are blown out and lit again, the roar of so many
people, yelling all the louder because they cannot move a limb, make
the sanest head swim. It seems impossible that the evening can end
without some serious injury, that the carriage horses will not get out
of hand, that many will not get bruised and crushed.

Still, in time, everyone begins to feel the need to get out of the throng, to reach the nearest side street or square and catch a breath of fresh air; the mass of people begins to melt away and this festival of universal freedom and licence, this modern Saturnalia, ends on a note of general stupefaction.

The common people are leaving in a great hurry to feast with relish on the meat which will be forbidden them after midnight, while the fashionable world goes to the various playhouses to bid farewell to the plays, which are cut very short this evening, for to these pleasures, too, the approaching hour of midnight will put an end.[21]

Jonson's play is the enactment of a day's carnival, which is only apparently brought to an end. In fact, it continues in the home of the figure of judgment whose original task is to criticize, restrain, and punish those excesses that are normal in a fair. Like Lovewit, but in a much more subtle and humane way, Adam Overdo enters the final scene to be absorbed by it. Unlike Lovewit he is no sudden interrupter of a festive trick. He is the constant misunderstanding observer of the amoral world of the fair. His project, which miserably fails, is to uncover its excesses and cheats. In this he is technically the figure on whose decision the timing of the end rests. His projected discovery, he imagines, will like a divine revelation expose everything and deal out punishment. Instead, because of his disguise, he becomes a figure of carnival himself. He is mocked and beaten and put in the stocks. At the end, his climactic discovery becomes a revelation and a recapitulation of his own compounded errors. Thus the would-be castigator of enormity becomes the initiator of celebration.

Through Overdo, Jonson tackles his least schematic and most many-sided movement towards ending in comedy. Overdo is an observer and a participant in a rich variety of action in a scene that is close to anarchy. This is because of the very nature of the fair, with its riff-raff, noise, and cheating. But it is also because he, Justice Overdo, has abdicated his responsibility as a judge in the Court of Pie Powder. There is no one before whom to bring offenders, for:

He is not to be found, Man. He ha' not been seen i' the *Fayre* here, all this liue-long day, neuer since seuen a clocke i' the morning.
(4.6.68–70)

Overdo's disguise is a weapon, but in his fool's habit he is simply another figure in the lively carnival scene:

They may haue seene many a foole in the habite of a Iustice; but neuer till now, a Iustice in the habit of a foole.
(2.1.7–9)

The play is the story of his unequal contest with this rich scene, which he fails to interpret, let alone change or judge.

The events that take place at the fair on the day of Cokes's visit are the amorphous material that Jonson shapes into a plot or into a series of parallel plots. But because the generating impulse is an occasion (the fair) rather than an aim, those plots do not push toward specific ends. The characters move into the ambience of the fair, are infected by it,[22] each in his own way, win or lose possessions and women, and then all gravitate towards the tawdry culminating spectacle of the puppet play and the scene of discovery.

The middle action of the play ties no knots like the deadlocks of romantic comedies, nor does it deepen any intrigue. It does, however, exemplify through each group the transformations worked by carnival, some of which Overdo observes and all of which present themselves for inclusion at the end.

The fair transforms but in fact isolates and magnifies the weakest qualities of those who succumb to its temptations. Thus Adam's disguise is that of a fool. This is only apparently topsy-turvy. Cokes, an idiot child to begin with, becomes more obviously so as he is stripped of his money, his clothes, and his bride. At the end he is left with his true delight, his toys, the puppets. He sums up his situation with unwitting clarity after being robbed when he meets the madman Troubleall:

> Friend, doe you know who I am? or where I lye? I doe not my selfe, I'll be sworne.
>
> (4.2.78–80)

Similarly, the respectable women, Mrs. Overdo and Mrs. Littlewit, are through drink and persuasion either treated like whores or offered the rewards of prostitution. The logic of carnival is an extreme one. It makes a mockery of nonlaughing carpers like Wasp by getting him drunk and put in the stocks. It makes of madness a quality that will gain the hand of a rich widow. It erupts again and again in the riot of absurd language (vapors) and obscene cursing and brawling (roaring). The events of this fair scene, then, specifically undermine the restraints of normal life by tempting and encouraging the appetites of the fair-goers with a gross and tawdry display of delights.

The most dangerous aspect of the fair's subversiveness is one that has great bearing on the possibilities of ending. It is subversive of law—not in the general sense that the carnival is a great opportunity for successful swindling, but specifically in the mockery, parody, and misuse of legal documents and language. As I shall show, Jonson dramatizes through Overdo the essentially absurd attempt to judge carnival by any laws but its own. But the mockery of legal apparatus in this setting is built into the plot through the strange adventures and meta-morphoses of a marriage license and a mysterious warrant.

Jonson's consciousness of license as a motif in his carnival play is apparent in his use of the word in the Epilogue spoken before King James at the one court performance of the play:[23]

> *Your* Maiesty *hath seene the* Play, *and you*
> *can best allow it from your eare, and view.*
> *You know the scope of* Writers, *and what store*
> *of* leaue *is giuen them, if they take not more,*
> *And turne it into* licence: . . .
>
> (1–5)

Making his plea before the court, Jonson adopts his responsible and magisterial manner. He makes the rational and socially acceptable dis-tinction, important as a defense of comedy, between allowed scope, store of leave, and license.[24] This distinction implies that there is a generous space in which the comic writer can move without approach-ing the dangerous extremes that would offend. But an epilogue at Court is one thing and the carnival experience of the play is another. If the Epilogue points to a respectable difference between scope and license, the play enacts the paradox in the word itself. At the beginning the marriage license of Cokes and Grace is snugly set in its black box, first in the Proctor's keeping and then handed over to the witless groom and his manservant Wasp. But this dry legal document of permission to marry gets caught up in the riotous scene of the fair and undergoes a transformation, like the characters. It is stolen in a scene of drunken brawling, the name on it is changed, and it moves from the possession of a fool and a carper to that of a wit (Quarlous). In short, legally approved permission is exploited, changed by and incorporated into the amoral license of the fair. Instead of a symbol of a solid citizen's financial and marital arrangements it becomes the means of enriching a fortune-hunting wit by sealing his projected marriage to the widow Purecraft. When Quarlous celebrates his victory over the guardian of the license at the end, he is celebrating the transformation of law by wit and making it impossible for the would-be judge (Overdo) to chastize the trick. License has become legal:

And carefull *Numps,* where's he? I thanke him for my licence.
                                                                        (5.6.88–89)

A variation of this transformation is the business of the warrant.[25] Through the anarchic scene with its perplexed and hiding judge who cannot decide when to reveal himself there wanders a madman, Troubleall. This is a man, himself once an official of the fair regulating court, dismissed by Overdo and gone mad as a result. His madness, the inability to conceive of any action unless it is approved by the "warrant" of Justice Overdo, is the reductio ad absurdum of the clash between law and carnival. Amidst the chaos of the fair, with its excesses and blatant disregard for law, there walks a man whose very bodily functions will not get done without legal approval:

> hee will doe nothing, but by Iustice *Ouerdoo*'s warrant, he will not eate a crust, nor drinke a little, nor make him in his apparell, ready. His wife, Sirreuerence, cannot get him make his water, or shift his shirt, without his warrant.
>
> (4.1.58–62)

Like *license, warrant,* a perfectly normal legal term, gets sucked into the madness of carnival. Pushed to the extreme, the legal form of approval loses all connection with reality and finally becomes a way of making the wit Quarlous rich. At the end of the play the fortune-hunting wit is in possession of the two legal documents. Both are transformed from specific permissions to blank checks. The name on the license is rubbed out and Overdo's warrant, given in error, is signed and sealed but open. Quarlous may write in it anything he likes:

> Looke thee! heere is my hand and seale, *Adam Ouerdoo,* if there be anything to be written, aboue in the paper, that thou want'st now, or at any time hereafter; thinke on't; it is my deed, . . .
>
> (5.2.116–19)

In both these cases the restrictive aspects of law have broken down before the onslaught of wit and madness. Law, which defines and limits, becomes license and an open warrant that is subject only to desire. Carnival then beats law at its own game, subverting it from within. It remains to be seen how Jonson's proclaimer of judgment and discovery, Adam Overdo, fares in his attempt to deal with "enormity."

As I have suggested above, "ending" in this play, which is not the urge to riot or the exhaustion of carnival itself, depends on the decision of the fool-judge Overdo. Right from the opening of the play he sets out his program, which is the discovery of enormity (a favorite word). It is a hopeless task, given the turbulence of carnival and the dullness of the judge. It is summed up with unconscious irony in Overdo's words:

> And as I began, so I'll end.
>
> (2.1.47–48)

He intends to begin and end as a figure of justice. He is much closer to beginning and ending as a fool, though finally a wiser one.

Through Overdo's career Jonson examines the notion of discovery in a way that is not characteristic of his usual comic style. Discovery in Jonson is usually the climactic pulling off of the mask. Like Volpone's unmasking or Epicoene's it is the gesture that breaks a plot open and spills its secrets. It may also be a revelation that lets the stage audience know how it has been tricked. In Overdo's case there is a culminating revelation but that is an anticlimax, and the structural emphasis is on the justice's misguided though honest attempts to discover for himself what he believes the fair to be hiding. Discovery is then a process rather than an act, a process that because of its pitfalls gives the benign and tolerant ending its authority.

Discovery can be said to be Overdo's humor. It is his passion as he wanders around, entering "enormities" into his black book. In the service of this passion he is beaten and put into the stocks. He once contemplates revelation to save himself a beating (3.3) but resolves with a display of absurd stoic gravity to endure:

> come infamy, come banishment, nay, come the rack, come the hurdle, (welcome all) I will not discouer who I am, till my due time;
>
> (3.3.37–39)

The discoveries that Overdo plans to use against carnival when he reveals himself are nearly all false or obvious. Thus it takes no elaborate disguise to "discover" the enormity of Ursula, the pig woman. Her enormity is physical:

> I am all fire, and fat, . . .
>
> (2.2.50)

Writing it down in a book is no way of curbing it. Similarly the rich slang and fluid scene of the fair are too complex for the moralizing judge-fool, and his discoveries are topsy-turvy ones. They are part of the carnival rather than judgments of it. Thus he takes the pickpocket Edgworth to be a proper young man in bad company, and the moralizing ballad about cutpurses sung by Nightingale to cover up robbery is taken by Overdo at its face value:

> It doth discouer enormitie, I'le marke it more: I ha' not liked a paltry piece of poetry, so well, a good while.
>
> (3.5.112–13)

These constant, repeated errors are the marks of Overdo's defeat by the fair, or more exactly, of his inability to save himself from its whirligig. Yet in his case carnival is also partly a clarifying experience. The stage image most directly opposed to discovery (as Overdo intends it) and most expressive of carnival confusion is the sight of Overdo in the stocks (4.1). The absurd pretensions of the invisible messenger of justice hiding in a cloud could not be exposed more obviously than by his suffering punishment for a crime he did not commit. Yet it is here that Jonson hints at another kind of discovery that is very pertinent to the ending. Overdo in the stocks hears the members of the watch discuss his reputation for severity on the bench:

> and when hee is angry, be it right or wrong; hee has the Law on's side, euer.
>
> (4.1.80–81)

This makes for a moment of grudging insight and reevaluation that is rare for a Jonsonian character:

> I will be more tender hereafter. I see compassion may become a *Iustice,* though it be a weaknesse, I confesse; and neerer a vice, then a vertue.
>
> (4.1.82–84)

But this remains a carnival play and Overdo's new tenderness is lavished on the disguised wit Quarlous instead of on the wronged Troubleall. So when the final interrupting revelation comes and Overdo descends "cloudlike" to

> break out in raine, and haile, lightning, and thunder, upon the head of enormity.
>
> (5.2.5–6)

this mock deus ex machina discovers his own frailty and nakedness rather than the excesses of the people he presumes to judge.

Like *A Midsummer Night's Dream,* the end of *Bartholomew Fair* includes a play that is the occasion for the gathering of all the major characters. Jonson's gross puppet play is an exposure of theater, comedy, and carnival in a much more extreme way than Shakespeare's mockery exposes bad actors and tearful tragedies in *Pyramus and Thisbe.* Shakespeare uses his play-within-the-play as a tool of ironic retrospection. Jonson uses his to create a grotesque mirror of all that is crudest about the fair and its pleasures. It is this miniature of concentrated crudity that is the ground for the penultimate battle between license and restraint and this battle, like Overdo's, ends in a discovery and a defeat.

The ending of *Bartholomew Fair* is composed of two consecutive and analogous sequences: the puppet play leading to Rabbi Busy's interruption and the discovery of Overdo leading to the curtain. The first is a replay in action of the basest aspects of carnival. The second is a review of what the fair has wrought in the lives of the central characters and an attempt at reaching a genial equilibrium. Taken together they offer the audience both an ironically subversive and a more socially acceptable version of the workings and purpose of comedy.

The puppet play is a travesty—one of the lowest kinds of comedy, which depends for its effect on a drastic cheapening of sublime material. Littlewit, like Jonson the comic poet, prides himself on choosing a local scene and characters:

> As for the *Hellespont* I imagine our *Thames* here; and then *Leander* I make a Diers sonne, about *Puddle-wharfe:* and *Hero* a wench o' the *Banke-side,* . . .
>
> (5.3.121–24)

The brainless author of this travesty has made it his aim to reduce the classical legend to the level of the lowest popular taste:

> I haue onely made it a little easie, and *moderne* for the times, Sir, that's all; . . .
>
> (5.3.120–21)

What is enacted, then, is a knockabout farce, spoken in the crudest Billingsgate, which imitates the basest aspects of the fair—its violence, noise, and animality.

The audience that gathers to watch this, "you of judgment," as Littlewit calls them, are the people on whom the carnival has wrought transformation and those who have exploited the fair. Apart from the pimps, rogues, wits, and the hidden judge, there are the idiot Cokes, the straying wives, and the shamed Wasp, the overseer whose "government" is at an end.

This is, then, a spectacle of misrule both on the puppet stage and in its audience. It is the lowest art, imitating a crude reality, displayed to an audience incapable of judgment. Comedy is here revealing its nakedness, its poor and common origins, and its shabby appeal to an unthinking audience. The play imitates base verbal and physical riot and it comes to an end in chaos as the puppets, swearing, knock each other about. True to comic tradition, riot is interrupted, first by a puppet, deus ex machina Dionysius, and then by the Puritan enemy of the stage, Rabbi Busy:

> Downe with *Dagon;* downe with *Dagon;* 't'is I, will no longer endure your prophanations.
>
> (5.5.1–2)

In the argument between Busy and the puppet Dionysius, Jonson ironically vindicates the crudest comedy and creates a culminating gesture of discovery that is both simple and obscene, a reductio ad absurdum of one of the most traditional motifs of ending.

Busy, the hypocritical foe of pleasure, fairs, and theaters, is defeated by being reduced to the level of the puppets. Jonson uses a learned pun to point to the common denominator between the puppets and the Puritan:

> *Quarlous:* I know no fitter match, then a *Puppet* to commit with an Hypocrite!
>
> (5.5.50–51)

Hypocrites is the Greek word for actor. Busy is a faker on the stage of the world.[26] In his arguments with Dionysius, Busy echoes the puppet and indeed, all the nonsense and noise of the fair and the puppet play:

> *Busy:*   It is prophane.
> *Puppet: It is not prophane.*
> *Busy:*   It is prophane.
> *Puppet: It is not prophane.*
>
> (5.5.71–74)

This is not argument but a cacophony of "base noise" and "treble creaking" that culminates in the puppet's discovery and Busy's silence and conversion.

When Dionysius "takes up his garment" to display his sexual neutrality, he not only refutes an old Puritan argument against actors but makes the ultimate defiant comic gesture. The revelation of nakedness and the display of sexual parts are significant elements in the oldest comedy of the Western tradition. In later times the display was transmuted into jokes about fatness, excretion, and the sexual members. Here the puppet ironically reveals a sexless wooden body, but the gesture remains triumphantly obscene. It is a vindication of the most primitive energies of comedy and yet, like more civilized discoveries, it solves the problem. Busy is convinced and becomes an assenting member of the comic audience. The play can go on:

> Let it goe on. For I am changed, and will become a beholder with
> you!
>
> (5.5.116–17)

Given this rowdy prologue it is no wonder that Overdo's discovery is
an anticlimax. The puppet has parodied it before it takes place, and
after Busy's interruption, Overdo's is déjà vu. Like Busy's, though in a
more humane way, Overdo's discovery is a reversal of the discoverer.
What professes to be an interruption and chastising of riot (enormity)
becomes an agreement to participate in it. Like the Puritan he is
changed by what he sees and becomes a member of the comic celebration.

Like a judge at the end of satire Overdo comes to bind and name the
wrongdoers. He calls the roll of names and his refrain is "stand there."
But his revelations are mistaken. He cannot tell the criminal from the
innocent or the madman from the wit. In unmasking he reveals himself
to have been a victim of masks. It is he who is fixed by Quarlous at the
end, not his "enormities":

> nay, Sir, stand not you fixt here, like a stake in *Finsbury* to be shot
> at, or the whipping post i' the *Fayre*, . . .
>
> (5.6.93–95)

Like Busy's false ranting against the stage, Adam's false judgment of
carnival excess is stopped by a crude physical gesture. His wife,
stuffed with food and drink, wants to be sick, and calls for his help:

> O lend me a bason, I am sicke, I am sicke; where's Mr. *Ouerdoo?*
>
> (5.6.67–68)

This display of animal weakness in his respectable wife finally puts
Adam where the play has always in fact had him, on a level with all the
other inhabitants of the comic world:

> remember you are but *Adam,* Flesh, and blood!
>
> (5.6.96–97)

Discovery in *Bartholomew Fair* is a way of mocking false judgment.
Carried as a threatening banner by Overdo as he observes the excesses
of the fair, it turns in the final confrontation into the revelation and
acceptance of a common frailty. The discoveries of this comedy, it
turns out, do not have much to do with judgment of a carping kind. The
wit Quarlous, for instance, profited from his discoveries at the fair. He

discovered a widow and a way of getting her money. This will be a subject of conversation with Overdo at the banquet after the play:

> There you and I will compare our *discoueries;* and drowne the memory of all enormity in your bigg'st bowle at home.
>
> (5.6.99–100)

So discovery becomes part of the geniality of carnival drinking and the comedy does not have to end. No one is expelled. All are included, even the puppets, those base comedians:

> *Cokes:* Yes, and bring the *Actors* along, wee'll ha' the rest o' the *Play* at home.
>
> (5.6.114–15)

The uniqueness of *Bartholomew Fair* in this quartet of Jonson's comedies is in its abandonment of the tightly closed plot built around a trick and a place that protects and symbolizes the trick. It is the fair that controls the action rather than any character, though the wits profit from it while the fools are fleeced and beaten. The fair includes all levels of humanity, indeed, animals and objects as well, and stresses what they have in common. The quirky metamorphoses of the trickster plays are here anchored in the low but natural variety of Smithfield. The naked puppet is Jonson's most suggestive revelation of the irreducible element in comedy. It is vulgar, childish, nonsensical, part of a low entertainment; yet its brash, animated display vindicates comedy as energy and fun. "Et sordet gesticulatio"—yes, but the drawn curtain and the full light make us, like Busy, spectators rather than critics.

4

Molière's Denouements

Galopin: Madame, on a servi sur table.
Dorante: Ah! voilà justement ce qu'il faut pour le
dénouement que nous cherchions. . . .
—*La Critique de l'École des femmes*

Jonson's comedies do not end in a stable way. Their anarchic material cannot be transformed into its opposite without miracles, and these do not occur in Jonson's world. At the most they end on a note of geniality that makes the world a fair or subversively turns us into accomplices in a cheat. The riotous behavior that kindles Jonson's imagination may be punished "by the law" in his satire, but he enlists the most primitive images (flesh and blood, the naked puppet) to establish the kind of base stability that is the closest he gets to a harmonious ending.

Molière's laconic endings do not so much state the achieved harmony of the group as the defeated or victorious condition of a single character who is outside the group. In a happy comedy like *Les Fourberies de Scapin,* which ends in multiple marriages, the symmetrically balanced couples of lovers and fathers occupy the background of the final tableau. It is Scapin, the trickster and fertile begetter of the plot, whose reappearance undoes the symmetry and steals the applause. It is his ending just as it was his comedy. This is even more clear in darker plays that focus on a defeated character. His consistency in defeat is likely to concentrate in it more of the play's meaning than the happiness of the lovers. Thus, Arnolphe's silent exit in *L'École des femmes,* like Alceste's in *Le Misanthrope,* is more than the defeat and explusion of a humor. Malvolio is a peripheral figure, and his exit is a point of darkness in the stable array of bright colors. Molière's defeated humors are the central characters of their plays. Their obsessions have peopled the stage and moved the action. It is necessary, then, that their defeat leave an emptiness behind, a sense of something

78

unresolved and permanent that is copresent with the lucky change in the fortunes of the lovers. (In this Morose's defeat is like that of Arnolphe in *L'École des femmes*.)[1]

The untying action is understated in Molière because his comedies are plays that enact situations of deadlock, repeating and intensifying them until, sometimes, a solution interrupts the pattern.[2] His emphasis on deadlock is such that in simple as well as complex plays the tied situation may never be untied, and the logic of the knot overcomes any expectations of release.[3] In the farcelike *George Dandin* the hero's degradation by his wife and her parents is a consistent pattern that no device of his can break. Similarly the logic of a grand obsession, like Alceste's sincerity, forces its repetition in more and more extreme situations till it finds release, ironically, in an exit from the social world. Only in those plays not dominated by an obsessed character does the artistry of untying bear as much weight as the state of impasse. In *Les Fourberies de Scapin,* for instance, the obsession happens to be that of the witty trickster, and it expresses itself in an itch to devise more and more elaborate devices of release.

The characteristic structure of Molière's comedies demonstrates a significant tension between the dominant pattern of repetition and the closing feature of discovery. In Shakespeare's comedies the emphasis on transformation and the possibility of change makes of discovery a climactic and often miraculous event. In plays like *The Tempest,* discovery is the rationale of the whole action and is summed up in its closing sequence. Even in Jonson's satirical drama discovery is a great flourish of ending *(Volpone, Epicoene)* or at least a device whose reinterpretation becomes a serious factor at the end *(Bartholomew Fair).*

The conventional scenes of recognition are of course found in Molière; bracelets reveal kinship and returning travelers put relationships right. But more significant is the way discovery is relegated to a subordinate position in the controlling pattern of repeated deadlock. *Tartuffe,* for example, is a play in which even the final revelation to Orgon of the hypocrite's baseness does not alter the legal trap that is the symbol of the knave's control of the house. Discovery does not, as in *Volpone,* break the deadlock. It leaves it intact, and only an intruder sent by the all-seeing king can untie the knot. Similarly, Arnolphe's discovery of the love between his locked-up innocent and Horace is the *basis* of the developing action in *L'École des femmes.* Discovery of the crucial fact conflicts with his voyeuristic obsession with finding out more and more, and is left unexploited till it is finally defeated. Its advantage is lost in the self-defeating logic of the jealous man's plot. Here the obsession (jealousy and the desire to know more) creates a

pattern of action that reverses the expectation of the opening discovery. For Arnolphe, as for George Dandin, knowledge is a trap.
Discovery is not in Molière a true motif of release, even when, as in *Le
Malade imaginaire,* it releases victims from the clutches of hypocrites
and fortune hunters. It cannot deal with the vitality of an obsession,
just as in *Tartuffe* it is helpless against the logic of a past mistake. In the
sick man's case, as in that of many of Molière's humors, the survival of
their obsession, its repetition in one form or another, balances the
conventional release that the end of the comedy affords the young
lovers.

The witty ending of the debate on comedy in *La Critique de L'École
des femmes* should not lead us to think that Molière was simply exploiting formulas in his denouements. The opposite is true. His use of
formulas is rarely the definitive factor at the end of his comedies, and
when they are used, they stand in ironic relationship to some far more
complex internal forces that may, as in *L'École des femmes,* have
already done their work for them. Our consciousness of pattern is far
more important at these endings than the interventions that
superficially allow them to finish. This pattern may be a jolly one of
trickery and bluff but it often is one of a repeated trap, in which case no
formula can really end it.

For a simple model of the happy pattern I take the early farce *Le
Médecin volant* and consider its complication in a comedy of trickery—*Les Fourberies de Scapin.* The simple model of the pattern of
deadlock is the farce *La Jalousie du Barbouillé,*[4] and its complication
can be studied in *George Dandin.*[5]

Le Médecin volant depends for its action and its complication solely
on its trickster character, Sganarelle. Presented with a problem to
enable the young lovers to meet, he has to decoy the obstructive
father, Gorgibus. The situation is a traditional one and its solution
flows naturally from the acrobatic mental and physical gifts of the
entertainer, Sganarelle. Caught by accident out of his doctor's disguise, in which he is decoying the father, he invents a brother whom he
now has to play as well as the doctor. The impossibility of being two
people in one place is a trap for Sganarelle and possible despair for the
lovers—the solution of the problem is the moving principle of the comedy to its end.

> *Sganarelle:* Mes affaires vont mal; mais pourquoi se désespérer?
> Puisque j'ai tant fait, poussons la fourbe jusques au
> bout. Oui, oui, il en faut encore sortir, et faire voir que
> Sganarelle est le roi des fourbes.

(14)

The pattern of incident is thus created both by the necessity of the situation (the lovers have to be saved) and the desire of the trickster to display his art flagrantly (jusques au bout). So the trickster plays both doctor and brother and all the obstacles thought of by the father's skeptical servant are overcome by Sganarelle's nimbleness.

This is, then, the kind of farcical tour de force that consumes itself. The trickster reaches a high point of agility after which his exposure is unimportant. The audience has been entertained and the lovers matched. Discovery is a danger only during the acrobatics; they are the raison d'être of the play and their successful completion coincides with its end.

In farces we need not take seriously the anger of the deluded father; in a more complicated play this is more of a factor and at the same time the acrobatics of the trickster are less obviously a concentrated physical exercise. However, the pattern remains remarkably constant in *Les Fourberies de Scapin*. Here the complications of the plot conceived by Scapin are an elaborate and hilarious way of achieving what fortune and accident achieve by themselves. The plot is a slightly more abstract version of the situation in *Le Médecin volant*. Instead of one pair of lovers and one father there are two of both, and instead of a "double" trickster there is only one, Scapin. But the logic of the action is the same—the invention of a series of tricks that will enable the young men to marry against the wishes of their fathers. Whereas Sganarelle's acrobatics are largely physical, Scapin's are verbal, as, for example, the invention of complicated lies to justify the extraction of money and promises from the reluctant fathers. Given the reluctant but final malleability of the old men and the resourcefulness of the joker, the pattern seems self-consistent, like Sganarelle's in the farce. But here Molière introduces discovery—not only to threaten but to break down the plot. Scapin has the itch of his type, here a weakness—the urge to push a device as far as possible, thus risking discovery and a beating:

Je me plais à tenter des entreprises hasardeuses.

(3.1)

His gratuitous device of the sack against the old man Géronte (3.2) has nothing to do with the plot but leads to the joker's discovery. In the very next scene the whole elaborate plot is accidentally exposed to the angry old man. But as usual in Molière, the revelation of the trick is not necessarily its defeat. Discovery here is of two kinds—the first kind which arouses anger exposes the elaborate action of the play as a series of tricks based on Scapin's lies. The second and more conventional kind (brought by the nurse) reveals the true identity of the forbidden girl and shows in retrospect that the deadlock and the turbulent action around it were based on nothing. There was never really a knot.

If there was something real at the core of the comedy it was the inventive wit, Scapin, who moved plots to both success and failure. His survival as an unrepentant joker is a counterweight to the symmetry of the fathers and lovers who have discovered that their complicated knot was nothing. Discovered as a liar, he ought to be punished by the stick he wielded against his master, Géronte. Instead, his reappearance at the end, swathed in bandages, a parody of an injured man, celebrates his triumph over punishment. Even death is a device for the Punchlike Scapin.

Ending in this play comes when the discovery of an elaborate trick, the moving principle of the plot, coincides with the formal recognitions that show the whole action to have been an energetic dance on one spot. The action was a gratuitous display causing laughter,[6] a vehicle in fact for Scapin, the character whose ethos is such a display.

The darker pattern concentrates on a victim figure and rejects discovery as a feature that contributes to ending. The victim in this pair of plays—*La Jalousie du Barbouillé* and *George Dandin*—is a deceived husband. His situation, both in the early farce and in the later play, is a fixed one, a trap from which there is no exit. The consistency of the comic pattern in the first two plays discussed was a consistency that promised release through the character whose ingenuity could work it. The consistency of the pattern in the latter two promises continuing deadlock. In this they are closer to Molière's great comedies of obsession.

The husband, Le Barbouillé, announces in the first speech of the farce that he is in a trap. Gross and miserable, he is married to a wife who is his enemy, but there is no way out:

> Ah! pauvre Barbouillé, que tu es misérable! Il faut pourtant la punir. Si je la tuais. . . . L'invention ne vaut rien, car tu serais pendu. Si tu la faisais mettre en prison . . . La carogne en sortirait avec son passepartout. Que diable faire donc?
>
> (1)

The figure of solution who presents himself at this question, Le Docteur, is a fake. Instead of suggesting a way out of the impasse he is instrumental in turning deadlock into riot. His "humor" of longwinded, nonsensical, philosophical tirades turns the conciliatory gathering of husband, wife, and her parents into a cacophony of noise:

Le Barbouillé, Angélique, Gorgibus, Cathau, Villebrequin parlent tous à la fois, voulant dire la cause de la querelle, et Le Docteur aussi, disant que la paix est une belle chose, et font un bruit confus de leurs voix; . . .

(6, stage direction)

The farce could end here, since this cacophony is an unmistakable expression of the ruling impasse. But such an ending would not focus on any single victim of the trap. Molière's comic logic does this by making discovery serve the deadlock. When Le Barbouillé chases his wife out of the house at night, the locked doors and his forthright dismissal of her seem to suggest a solution:

Le Barbouillé: Adieu! *Vade retro, Satanas.*

(11)

But her ruse of playing dead, his exit from and her recapture of the house, reverse the discovery. It remains the useless knowledge of the deceived husband. The parents arrive to find him outside the house, accused of drunkenness and violence. His isolation is complete and his only appeal is to the audience:

Le Barbouillé: Je me donne au diable, si j'ai sorti de la maison, et demandez plutôt à ses Messieurs qui sont là-bas dans le parterre; c'est elle qui ne fait que de revenir. Ah! que l'innocence est opprimée!

(12)

The crude husband is a figure of farce, and sentiment is not in place here. *We* certainly cannot save him from the impasse of his marriage. The laconic ending is a display of the absence of resolution by its very use of the language of accord. The Doctor, woken up by the quarrel, wants to know what it is about:

Villebrequin: Ce n'est rien, Monsieur le Docteur; tout le monde est d'accord.

(13)

The traditional resolutions of jovial comedy—accord and pardon—are ironically paraded here to stress their irrelevance. What survives is the impasse of the marriage, clarified by the knockabout action and intensified by the reversal of discovery.

The subordination of discovery to the logic of repeated impasse is apparent in the more substantial and emotionally involving play, *George Dandin*. The fundamental situation of the farce is here made more socially specific. The characters are no longer just masks in certain family relationships to each other, but belong to specific social classes. Thus the conflict between husband and wife is deepened by the fact that she, the daughter of a genteel family, has been married off against her wishes to a rich peasant. Her disgust with her common husband and readiness to entertain the courtship of a fashionable lover arise out of her anger at being caught in the trap of a loveless marriage:

> *Angélique:* M'avez-vous, avant le mariage, demandé mon consente-
> ment, et si je voulais bien de vous? Vous n'avez
> consulté, pour cela, que mon père et ma mère; ce sont
> eux proprement qui vous ont épousé, et c'est pourquoi
> vous ferez bien de vous plaindre toujours à eux des torts
> que l'on pourra vous faire.
>
> (2.2)

The situation of impasse is thus seen from the point of view of the wife as well as that of the victim protagonist. Yet the cumulative logic of the repeatedly foiled discovery focuses a sharp and cruel light on the husband whose isolation can be known only to us.

Dandin is a man in search of public corroboration of his isolated discovery (1.2) that his wife is unfaithful. He is not an obsessively jealous man nor is he painted as a monster of suspicion. He is, however, obsessed with gaining belief for his discovery, which means nothing until it can be witnessed and made real by the presence of his wife's father and mother:

> si le galant est chez moi, ce serait pour avoir raison aux yeux du père
> et de la mère, et les convaincre pleinement de l'effronterie de leur
> fille.
>
> (2.6)

The major action of the play is devoted to Dandin's ever more desperate efforts to prove himself wronged and to find justification in the eyes of the parents-in-law, the aristocratic Sotenvilles. This is from the outset a hopeless task. The parents are blinded by the light of their aristocratic name; prisoners of that obsession, they are no judges of reality. Angélique, his wife, and her lover, Clitandre, are too clever to be trapped. Dandin, who will be understood by no one and can express himself freely only in soliloquy, is at the end reduced to the silence that completes his trap.

Dandin is the direct opposite of the comic tricksters of the happy farces. He is the initiator of plots that fail, and instead of tying up his enemies, he ties himself up. His career in the play is mapped out through the repetition of three failed discoveries. Each failure ends with an act of degradation that is the defeat of his hope that discovery will justify him. In each case his witnesses (the parents) see the reverse of the truth and take the initiative in decreeing the form of his debasement.

The first attempt (1.5.6) founders on the flat denials of the courtier, the wife, and her servant. Dandin's inability to prove his charges turns the trap he wished to set against himself:

J'enrage de bon coeur d'avoir tort, lorsque j'ai raison.

(1.6)

As a man who has made the crucial discovery he sees clearly the full absurdity of his position—having to accept the denial of a liar:

Voulez-vous que je sois serviteur d'un homme qui me veut faire cocu?

(1.6)

But Dandin's clarity is not that of his audience and he is forced to beg pardon of his wife's courtier. Each instance of failed proof, separated from the preceding one by Dandin's false hope of corroboration, makes more extreme the protagonist's isolation as a possessor of truth. After each act of debasement (the second is a beating—2.8), the parents see the case as closed. His deadlock is their acceptable ending:

Madame de Sotenville: Je suis ravie de voir vos désordres finis et des transports de joie que vous doit donner sa conduite.

(2.8)

To this Dandin's answer is, "Je ne dis mot," though the moving principle of the plot, his hopeless search for justification, overcomes his silence once more.

Knowledge isolates George Dandin. The limited number of characters are hostile; basically the husband, the wife, the courtier, and the parents seal the situation against the kind of intervention that might split it open. The repetition of foiled discovery is a structure that creates a kind of comic necessity acted out in plot but rooted in the unnatural marriage between a peasant and the daughter of gentry.

The final reversal of discovery (3.6, 7, 8) is the most graphic as spectacle and the most troubling emotionally. It is different from the others because Dandin at first succeeds. The straying wife is locked out of the house. It is also different in that the husband and wife engage in a longer dialogue than at any other moment in the play. This dialogue is a refinement, a translation into terms of feeling, of the deadlock between them. She tempts him with a confession of her wrongdoing, asks for his pardon, and allows him the sense of being right:

> Il est vrai que j'ai failli, je vous l'avoue encore une fois, et que votre ressentiment est juste;
>
> (3.6)

This is the truth but its aim is to foil discovery. In the same way her appeal to his tolerance is met with a flat "Non." In farce feeling is not allowed to complicate absurd or gross conflicts. Here the situation, borrowed from farce, is penetrated with feeling, which even if it is a pretense (her confession), fleshes out the emotional impasse that is their marriage. His "Non" is logical, though a "Oui" would change nothing. The fact is that neither answer can alter the necessity of Dandin's defeat. Given the pattern, change is impossible.

The final reversal of discovery brings the parents to find Dandin outside the house and the triumphant wife within it. He is reduced almost to incoherence:

> Jamais . . . Peut-on . . . Madame, je vous prie . . . Souffrez que je vous . . .
>
> (3.7)

Then he has to submit to the crowning indignity of going down on his knees before his wife to ask her pardon. Dandin alone on the stage at the end sums up in his very presence defeat and isolation. The trap cannot be sprung, and the only way out is to flee—"je le quitte" (3.8)—perhaps to death—"s'aller jeter dans l'eau la tête la première" (3.8).[7]

In this rigorous plot there is neither a tying or an untying action. A situation existing at the opening is pushed to its extreme. Unlike the farce the play imitates, the relationships, especially that of husband and wife, are given a more than minimal emotional weight. But like the farce, the logic of the repeated reversal is one that subordinates feeling. Dandin is the opposite of Scapin, the comic trickster. Although they both occupy the stage at the end and have initiated the repeated devices of their plays, the devices of Scapin work release, while those of Dandin create traps. Scapin works hard to avoid discovery but when it comes it does not defeat him. Dandin works hard to proclaim discovery, and this very labor defeats him. They are the opposite poles of Molière's comic world. He was as interested in the patterns of defeat as he was in those of victory. In Jonson's comedies the trickster and the victim are usually coupled in conflict; the victory of the wit subordinates the defeat of the dupe. Molière, in isolating the victim and building a comedy on his defeat, is a more honest and disturbing comic artist. He accepts the maliciousness in laughter and does not compensate for it by giving his audience something to feel decently jovial about.[8] Moreover, by making his victim a bearer of knowledge from the start, he alters the bias of traditional comic actions. These begin with ignorance or false knowledge and move towards their punishment or transformation by the revelation of the truth. Here knowledge is punished ironically, as if it were an eccentricity—which it is, in a society that declares as normal the state of being deceived.

Central features of the victim farces and those of the trickster plays combine in *L'École des femmes* to make that spare and concentrated masterpiece an outstanding example of the integration of pattern and theme. Its ending superficially is brought about by the intervention of Enrique, the *persona ad catastrophem machinata,* whose name and history are carefully planted early on in the play. His is the conventional discovery that clarifies the status of Arnolphe's locked-up ward, Agnès, and his arrival brings parental approval to the love affair between her and the young Horace. But these discoveries are only a public affirmation of an end that has actually been achieved in a far more complicated and ironic way through an intense battle between two men (Arnolphe and Horace) whose status as trickster and victim and whose exploitation and ignorance of discovery are major elements in a pattern that pointedly calls attention to itself as essence as well as structure.

In *La Critique de L'École des femmes* Molière himself draws attention to the structural peculiarities of his play. The rival poet Lysidas faults the comedy for its lack of action:

> et dans cette comédie-ci, il ne se passe point d'actions, et tout consiste en des récits que vient faire ou Agnès ou Horace.
>
> (6)

Uranie, who is favorable to the play, defends this lack of action by pointing out how it is just this structure of confidences that is the basis for the ironic pattern which leads to Arnolphe's final reversal:

> et ce qui me paraît assez plaisant, c'est qu'un homme qui a de l'esprit, et qui est averti de tout par une innocente qui est sa maîtresse, et par un étourdi qui est son rival, ne puisse avec cela éviter ce qui lui arrive.
>
> (6)

Uranie's answer contains the essence of the play's nuclear situation:

the possessor of knowledge, Arnolphe, "averti de tout," his victims, who lack knowledge, "une innocente, un étourdi," and the comic necessity that makes it impossible for Arnolphe to exploit his knowledge for his own ends.

This necessity is set out with a logic that reminds us of Jonson in *The Alchemist*—though the severe limitation on the number of characters makes for a far greater concentration on one conflict. The setting is simple, in essence a vehicle for a naked, farcelike action. There is a house with a girl locked up in it—its treasure. That is the action's pivot. Around it, in a narrow space, move two men. The older is conscious of the struggle, and the younger is unaware, revealing each of his moves to his worst enemy. In simple farces based on errors of identity *(The Comedy of Errors)* the characters suffer a democracy of ignorance. They are all equally subject to the errors forced on them by the plot. The resolving moment of recognition, therefore, comes when they meet—a moment to be avoided for as long as the comedy has to last. Here, in a manner typical of Molière's comic method, Arnolphe discovers his rival *before* the action has properly got under way (1.4). This partial recognition is the basis rather than the end of the intrigue. Such a point of departure does not rule out the typically accelerating hide-and-seek action of farces of error, though we are *told* of such sequences and do not see them. Horace narrates to Arnolphe how he was nearly caught in Agnès's room by Arnolphe himself (4.6). However, the fact that discovery is an opening gambit of the play crucially affects its tenor.

Knowledge imposes a burden of action on the knower, and Arnolphe is anyway the initiator of the play's action. His first speech looks forward to the end (marriage) for which he has been preparing his innocent ward:

> Oui, je veux terminer la chose dans demain.
>
> (1.1.2)

This end, like Morose's project of marriage in *Epicoene,* is inherently unnatural. For a man obsessed with cuckoldry, to marry is to risk reversal, as Arnolphe's friend, the raisonneur Chrysalde points out:

> Oui; mais qui rit d'autrui
> Doit craindre qu'en revanche on rie aussi de lui.
>
> (1.1.45–46)

But Arnolphe is an obsessed character whose fear of cuckoldry and obsession with secrecy and spying make it impossible for him to exploit his discovery to defeat his rival. The comic necessity of the play that ensures his reversal, despite his initial advantage, is thus rooted in the character whose obsession compels him to delay revelation until he has brought about the very end he was trying to prevent. This is the self-consistency of plot praised by Uranie in the *Critique*. Essentially, it is the trap prepared by Arnolphe for himself.

The turning of discovery into a trap for the discoverer is clearly marked in Arnolphe's soliloquy at the end of 1.4. This is a crucial moment of decision, for the discovery could be rationally exploited to spoil Hector's chances. The plot could end here with revelation and the physical removal of the girl. Instead, Arnolphe's desire to find out more, a function of his obsession with cuckoldry, sets out the probable sequence for the rest of the play:

> *Arnolphe:* Mais ayant tant souffert, je devais me contraindre
> Jusques à m'éclaricir de ce que je dois craindre,
> À pousser jusqu'au bout son caquet indiscret,
> Et savoir pleinement leur commerce secret.
>
> (1.4.363–66)

Here is the obsessed man attempting to play the trickster's game. When Sganarelle in *Le Médecin volant* uses the phrase "poussons la fourbe jusques au bout" (14), he is speaking as a free inventor of entertaining comic devices. Arnolphe is talking of pushing to its end a device that can only cause him more knowledge and pain.

Knowledge is Arnolphe's trap as it is that of George Dandin, though it gives Arnolphe at least the illusion of taking action to achieve his aims. The structure of separate interviews with his intended bride and the young man are scenes of torture in which the jealous interrogator of the lovers becomes the repository of information that angers and pains him as he seeks it:

> *Agnès:* Il jurait qu'il m'aimait d'une amour sans seconde,
> Et me disait des mots les plus gentils du monde,
>
> . . . .
>
> *Arnolphe (à part)* Ô fàcheux examen d'un mystère fatal,
> Où l'examinateur souffre seul tout le mal!
>
> (2.5.559–60, 565–66)

His accidental discovery of their attraction for each other thus becomes an extended isolated observation of the progress of the love affair and of the miraculous change it has worked on the woman he had wished to fix in his own sterile image:

Horace: Il le faut avouer, l'amour est un grand maître:
Ce qu'on ne fut jamais il nous enseigne à l'être;
Et souvent de nos moeurs l'absolu changement
Devient, par ses leçons, l'ouvrage d'un moment; . . .
(3.4.900–903)

A dramatic style that hides the act and displays its narration and interpretation is a perfect vehicle for the apparent deadlock occupying the center of the play, and for the inevitable movement towards recognition and release that underlies this deadlock.

The action going on off the stage is violent and farcical. Arnolphe rages and breaks the china (4.6); he almost catches Horace in Agnès's room (4.6); Horace gets beaten and left for dead (5.1). But what we see and hear are the apparently calm conversations in which all this ineffective violence and turbulence are described by Horace to his enemy. The deadlock that this conveys is only superficially that of a contest that can move neither way successfully. Fundamentally it is the frustration of Arnolphe who is the initiator of all the violent action. This action, aimed at discovery and victory, keeps returning the actor to the position from which he started. Its violence is always belied by its result. Thus Arnolphe is certain that the attack on Horace left him dead rather than injured:

Ciel! dans quel accident me jette ici le sort!
Et que puis-je résoudre à voir cet homme mort?
(5.2.1358–59)

But this is followed by the entry of Horace telling the story of his lucky escape. The trap of knowledge is thus intensified for Arnolphe by the failure of all action that issues from that knowledge. Absurdly, those actions do not even succeed in breaking down his isolation to the extent of revealing to Horace that his "confidant" is his enemy.

The height of deadlock and the height of riot coincide in this play to force the final sequence of discovery. The discoveries of act 5 subordinate the isolated knowledge of Arnolphe and the ignorance of Horace and Agnès to the external pattern of the story. The interventions from outside split open the claustrophobic world of the plot and bring news of romance, disaster, and accident that change nothing but authorize and give fortune's sanction to what the inner action has achieved independently.

The formal denouement introduced by the entry of Enrique is preceded by a series of discoveries that make the ruling impasse physically and verbally explicit without suggesting a way out. The secret of the play—the true relationship between the three protagonists—has been the artfully hidden pivot of all the action. The intrigue that knits the three so tightly together keeps them artificially separate, holding the moment of their meeting in abeyance as a probable moment of recognition. But unlike the similar structural goal of a simpler play like *The Comedy of Errors,* meeting itself is not the key to general recognition. It is the absence of discovery that is behind the physical image which sums up the ferociously consistent tangle of *L'École des femmes.* The sight (5.3) of Horace handing over Agnès to the safekeeping of his "friend" Arnolphe to save her from the violence and jealousy of her guardian is the whole conflict exposed in a group of gestures. There is the violence of the guardian: *"Arnolphe la tire,"* the trusting ignorance of Horace:

> N'appréhendez rien:
> Entre de telles mains vous ne serez que bien, . . .
> (5.3.1474–75)

and there is the fear and reluctance of the woman between them. It is also an image of deadlock masquerading as release. Agnès has been smuggled out of the locked room only to be returned to the hands of her jailer. The narrow confines of the plot depend upon this close cooperation between knowledge and ignorance. It can survive absurdly on the edge of discovery as in 5.3 but it begins to break apart when powerful feelings contained hitherto by the necessities of pretense burst out in moments of direct confrontation.

In 5.4 Arnolphe unmasks: "Me connaissez-vous?", he says, revealing himself to Agnès as her "new protector." But this is more than a physical unmasking; it marks the end of Arnolphe's role as a spy and announces his attempt to claim her as a lover. The extreme quality, the explicitness of the confessions and denials of love in this scene of discovery are noted as distasteful by Lysidas in the *Critique:*

> *Lysidas:* Et ce Monsieur de La Souche enfin, qu'on nous fait un homme d'esprit, et qui paraît si sérieux en tant d'endroits, ne descend-il point dans quelque chose de trop comique et de trop outré au cinquième acte, lorsqu'il explique à Agnès la violence de son amour, avec ces roulements d'yeux extravagants, ces soupirs ridicules, et ces larmes niaises qui font rire tout le monde?
>
> (6)

Lysidas is a hostile critic but he directs attention to the unique status of the explosion of plain speech, however grotesque, in a play that has built up its tensions by a consistent evasion of direct confrontations.

Arnolphe, pushed to the extreme, is a figure in whom deadlock and riot coexist to the point of madness. In his lover's fit he turns into the opposite of the cramped disciplinarian he has been throughout the play. He will let her do anything:

> Je te bouchonnerai, baiserai, mangerai;
> Tout comme tu voudras, tu pourras te conduire:
> Je ne m'explique point, et cela, c'est tout dire.
>   (5.4.1595–97)

But fourteen lines later he is condemning her, on her refusal, to the most locked-up condition his imagination can conceive:

> Vous rebutez mes voeux et me mettez à bout,
> Mais un cul de convent me vengera de tout.
>   (5.4.1610–11)

Discovery thus remains a trap until the very last scene. The lonely advantage of Arnolphe's knowledge at the beginning and the passionate self-revelation of his confession of love at the end are the entrance and the blocked exit of the trap that is the elaboration in dramatic situations of his own frozen and sterile nature. True to himself until the very end is his misuse of his knowledge to force Horace's father to press the young man's marriage to the very girl he has locked away forever. That was the one thing he could not know:

> *Oronte:* —vous avez chez vous celle dont il s'agit, . . .
>   (5.9.1735)

The figures in the scene of denouement use words like "hasard" and "mystère" to describe the coincidence of Agnès's being the love of Horace, the daughter of Enrique and the ward of Arnolphe. But accident or mystery are the least significant factors in the completion of this action, just as the narration of the prehistory of the plot is in fact irrelevant to its self-consistency. This consistency is the result of the endurance of the opening situation as a structural motif. Essentially this situation is only exhausted seventy lines before the end when Horace discovers who Arnolphe really is. Its pattern is in abstract, the infinitely repeatable one of a kind of knowledge and a kind of ignorance that neutralize each other.

The play's foregrounding of narration and subordination of action increase the impression of the impossibility of movement. But the impasse of the conflict is undermined by the emotions that it fosters and ultimately cannot restrain. Discovery is given to Arnolphe at the start as a weapon but he uses it at the end to tear himself open. His failure to exploit it is consistent with his obsession with knowing. This begins as a passion and ends as a torture, from which his silent exit can be no release.

Arnolphe's plot is self-consuming, a pattern of his unnatural obsession with his own and others' secrets. He never moves out of the narrow confines of the circle at the center of which Agnès is kept like a hoard of gold. His last moves, which press the marriage of Horace to Enrique's daughter, are his attempt to close the pattern his way; instead they complete it in a reversed way. The interruptions of the outside world explain the pattern as part of a story, but they add nothing to the necessity of Arnolphe's defeat, which is accomplished by himself.

Tartuffe is not content to stay within the confines of the household over whose government he has gained unnatural control. His progress in the play, unlike Arnolphe's, is not around one object but is a seemingly inevitable movement toward the amassing of more and more power. This goes as far as the king, to whom Tartuffe turns as an informer, and it consequently brings about the most controversial denouement in Molière's work:[9] the intervention of the royal power to untie the knot that mortal efforts failed to loosen.

The earliest commentaries on the play, even from writers friendly to Molière, are divided on the question of the justice of the denouement. The anonymous author of the *Lettre sur la comédie de l'Imposteur* (1667),[10] writing under the probable guidance of Molière himself, defends the ending mainly on the grounds of its majestic vraisemblance. He admits that the state of Orgon's family in act 5 is one of ". . . la dernière désolation, par la violence et l'impudence de l'imposteur".[11] There seems to be no way out short of divine intervention. He then praises the aptness of the device of royal intervention, calling it "magnifique" and "merveilleux," as well as the contradictory qualities "naturel" and "juste." However, the reason for its success, according to the writer, are the qualities of the king rather than the artistry of the poet. The king is the perfect agent of discovery because he is gifted with "cette plénitude de lumière, cette prodigieuse pénétration d'espirit, et ce discernment merveilleux de toutes choses."[12] In short, where others are blind, he sees.

Boileau, on the other hand, found Molière's ending too serious: ". . . elle laisse le spectateur dans le tragique."[13] He suggested, according to his friend Claude Brossette, a farcelike scene of domestic judgment as a more fitting and comic end to the play. This would have left Tartuffe at the mercy of the family, who would have beaten him with the traditional "bâton" of the farces. In addition, Boileau, more true to Molière than Molière himself, would have ended the comedy on a note of failed discovery and ensured the absurd survival of a duped character. Madame Pernelle, consistent to the end in her faith, would refuse to believe in Tartuffe's guilt:

> Enfin Madame Pernelle seroit venue; elle auroit fait le diable à quatre pour soutenir l'honneur et la vertu de son cher Tartuffe: la scène auroit été belle; on auroit pu lui faire dire bien des choses sur lesquelles le parterre auroit éclaté de rire: elle auroit querellé le parterre et se seroit retirée en grondant, ce qui auroit fini agréablement la comédie.[14]

Both Molière in his actual ending[15] and Boileau in his suggestion turn from the self-contained action of the stage to the world beyond. Molière turns to the king, the source of indisputable discovery and justice. Boileau would moderate the finality of this by turning to the audience, who are also judges, but merry ones. They are entertained as much by the spectacle of obstinate and argumentative absurdity (Mme. Pernelle) as they are satisfied by the display of elementary comic justice (the beating of Tartuffe).

The difference between the two endings is based on the difference between the most rigorous universal satire and a comedy of essentially domestic ridicule.

Satire is an art of aggression against formidable figures of evil. It achieves its aims by exposing them in grotesque detail, but its plot is often the narration or enacting of how they defeat discovery. Molière in his *Préface* defends his art against critics by emphasizing its success in uncovering vice and exposing it to ridicule:

> C'est une grande atteinte aux vices que de les exposer à la risée de tout le monde. (p. 885)

This may be the aim of satire, but it is not its method. This method, and this is clearly demonstrated in *Tartuffe,* is to display vice in its capacity of subverter of a world, to push this subversion to the edge of disaster and only then defeat it. The weight of the action is on the *success* of the knave and the collaboration of his dupe, who is far more a figure of ridicule than the hypocrite. The consistency of this collaboration is repeatedly put to the test of discovery. But even when Tartuffe is exposed to Orgon, the logic of the collaboration between knave and dupe is not broken. The consequences of Tartuffe's subversion of the household remain intact. Indeed the satirical assumptions of Molière's plot lead to the ineffective discovery of act 4 and make the appeal outside the play to royalty inevitable.

Two major lines of the plot, focusing on the two protagonists, lead to two contrasting moments of climactic discovery. The first line is that of the dupe, Orgon. The subject is an infatuation and how it is overcome. The second is that of the knave Tartuffe. Its subject is the usurpation of power and its defeat. The first subject is a personal and domestic one; its bounds are the bourgeois family and its property. The second begins in the family unit but would expand beyond its confines into the society about it. Orgon's discovery is the result of a traditional device of comedy. Tartuffe's defeat is a project that no trick of comedy can accomplish. Ridicule, despite Molière's claims in his *Préface,* is not a strong enough weapon against the combination of vice and power.[16]

The disabusing of Orgon, the true subject of the play, according to the *Lettre sur la comédie de l'Imposteur,* is a project untypical of Molière's comedy in its demonstration of the victory of reason over an obsession. However, by twice linking discovery with deadlock Molière subordinates the revelations that would defeat Tartuffe to the weaknesses in Orgon upon which the knave thrives. Molière's entire oeuvre suggests to us that he is not interested in dramatizing the unambiguous awakening of an infatuated man. In his comedies characters are commonly disabused by being defeated, like Arnolphe, and remaining essentially what they were when the action began. Orgon is untypical in his change (the *Lettre* calls it "merveilleux")[17] but by comparing the two analogous sequences of domestic discovery (3.6 and 7; 4.6, 7, and 8), one may observe how the repetition draws discovery twice into the pattern created by the illusion that is stronger than it.[18]

Both sequences are a summation, by means of a simple stage device—a concealed listener—of a peculiar tension in the play between the successful hypocrisy of its protagonist and his transparency. Tartuffe is an obvious fake from the beginning of the play. He is labelled as such by all the sane members of the household. The fact that he does not appear in the first two acts makes it possible for Molière to use the most direct language of analysis and exposure. Thus Dorine says of Tartuffe:

Lui, qui connaît sa dupe et qui veut en jouir,
Par cent dehors fardés a l'art de l'éblouir;
Son cagotisme en tire à toute heure des sommes,
Et prend droit de gloser sur tous tant que nous sommes.
(1.2.199–202)

The transparency of the knave stops short, of course, before the one person who could give it practical effect, Orgon. Even he exposes him, in his "portrait" of Tartuffe, but he is blind to the significance of the damning picture of calculated piety that he draws:

> Il attirait les yeux de l'assemblée entière
> Par l'ardeur dont au Ciel il poussait sa prière;
> Il faisait des soupirs, de grands élancements,
> Et baisait humblement la terre à tous moments; ... .
>
> (1.5.285–88)

The necessity of discovery, then, is not simply a necessity of plot, which in these early acts is the attempt to block the knave's marriage to Mariane. It is the only way out of the grotesque situation in which the knowledge shared by an entire household is rendered ineffective by the blindness of its head.

The state of affairs in Orgon's house is thus similar to that in *George Dandin,* with a shift of emphasis in the relative positions of the isolated character and the group. In the farce the isolated character is the gross victim bearing knowledge that he cannot make real to the group. In *Tartuffe* the group of reasonable people is paradoxically isolated because it bears knowledge that it cannot make real to the madman who has the authority.

The set-up scene of discovery, that ancient trick of the stage, is thus a concentration into a series of gestures (preparing the trap, tempting the victim, discovery, and denunciation) of the attempts of the rational people to break out of their isolation. However, its failure only deepens that isolation.

The first sequence of discovery is not intended as such by its main plotters. Its purpose is to use Elmire as bait to block Tartuffe's match with Mariane. But the urge to expose the hypocrite, which is built into the deadlocked situation, finds its expression in the irascible Damis. Dorine warns of the possible failure of the rational project (stopping the marriage) if the young man is pushed by anger to force a discovery:

> *Damis:* Je ne lui dirai rien.
> *Dorine:* Vous vous moquez: on sait vos transports ordinaires,
>   Et c'est le vrai moyen de gâter les affaires.
>   Sortez.
>
> (3.1.848–51)

Discovery, though a rational aim, is in this specific context given an irrational basis—Damis's anger and his inability to bide his time. Damis wants to use discovery to force an ending. He thanks God:

> Pour m'ouvrir une voie à prendre la vengeance
> De son hypocrisie et de son insolence,
> À détromper mon père, et lui mettre en plein jour
> L'âme d'un scélérat qui vous parle d'amour.
>
> (3.4.1025–28)

But the violence of the discoverer is neutralized by the contradictory violent disbelief of the infatuated man, and the truth is turned into an aberration:

> Ah! traître, oses-tu bien par cette fausseté
> Vouloir de sa vertu ternir la pureté?
>
> (3.6.1087–88)

Earlier examples from *Volpone* and *The Alchemist* showed that the logic of knave/dupe situations can turn a moment of discovery into its opposite. Surly's attempt to expose the tricksters in *The Alchemist* is drowned in noise, and the display of the sick Volpone in court boldly mocks the gesture and language of exposure. Tartuffe also parodies discovery as he deprives the names that would define his evil of their power by using them cunningly against himself:

> Oui, mon frère, je suis un méchant, un coupable,
> Un malheureux pécheur, tout plein d'iniquité, . . .
>
> (3.6.1074–75)

This fake denunciation tightens the knot of illusion instead of untying it. Like Surly, Damis is expelled, leaving the knave more securely in control than before. The tours de force of Jonson's tricksters are played out in a world peopled almost entirely by dupes. Tartuffe's victories are more threatening because they are won in a realistically drawn society of reasonable people. The failure of the first discovery is to a certain extent due to the reticence of the eminently reasonable wife, Elmire, who is reluctant to add her voice to the denunciation. Her moderation is advanced by Orgon later in the play as an argument against the truth of his son's accusation:

> Vous étiez trop tranquille enfin pour être crue
> Et vous auriez paru d'autre manière émue.
>
> (4.3.1321–22)

This moderation is Elmire's conscious ideology, and it is both a weak link in the fight to expose Tartuffe and an important factor in the final success of the battle.

Its weakness lies in treating the conflict with the hypocrite as a private affair, a question of the tactful rejection of a man's advances by a faithful but not prudish wife. Her rule—"On ne doit d'un mari traverser le repos" (3.5.1068)—is a rule of the comedy of manners but not of satire. In a play in which all the sane characters struggle desperately to wake Orgon out of his sleep she adopts a strangely delicate, almost neutral stance. She is against the brusqueness of unmasking. She refuses to see the house as a battlefield, and her refusal contributes directly to the survival of the knave. However, this very moderation becomes in 4.3 the basis of Orgon's agreement to set up another trap of discovery:

> *Elmire:* Il faut que par plaisir, et sans aller plus loin,
>   De tout ce qu'on vous dit je vous fasse témoin.
> *Orgon:* Soit: je vous prends au mot.
>
> (4.3.1351–53)

Elmire's lack of extremism, her subtle preparation of the plot, make this second attempt at discovery different in quality from the first. In her speech of instruction to Orgon, already ridiculously under the table, she restates the aims of discovery in an enlightening way. She warns her husband of the explosive content of the situation—"Quoi que je puisse dire, il doit m'être permis" (4.4.1371)—subordinating this dangerous content to the aim of the plot—"Faire poser le masque à cette âme hypocrite" (4.4.1374). But the all-important emphasis is on the restoration of manliness to Orgon. The situation is farcical in its physical arrangement. The husband, listening to the insulting remarks of his "friend," punctuated by the coughs and kicks of his wife, is in the painful position of the dupe becoming aware of his folly. But the gross situation is refined by Elmire's emphasis on Orgon's assuming the responsibility of stopping the frenzy of the tempted man:

> J'aurai lieu de cesser des que vous vous rendrez,
> Et les choses n'iront que jusqu'où vous voudrez.
> C'est à vous d'arrêter son ardeur insensée,
> Quand vous croirez l'affaire assez avant poussée,
> D'épargner votre femme, et de ne m'exposer
> Qu'à ce qu'il vous faudra pour vous désabuser:
> Ce sont vos intérêts; vous en serez le maître, . . .
>
> (4.4.1379–85)

Elmire's speech makes Orgon into a fully conscious agent of discovery, reversal, and ending. The situation is engineered to force him to consider the question "how far?"—a question his infatuation did not allow him even to conceive. It gives him the opportunity to be again the master of his own interests by taking the simple steps of emerging from his hiding place, defending his wife, and expelling the culprit.

But the didactic and optimistic clarity of this project is in conflict with the real consequences of the blindness that the discovery aims to cure. Orgon, forced by his wife into seeing the truth and taking responsibility for his fate ("maître") is the man who has given up the mastery of his own house and property. The fatal gift, decided upon in the aftermath of the first failed discovery, returns to cancel the results of the second successful discovery. The mastery is Tartuffe's:

> C'est à vous d'en sortir, vous qui parlez en maître:
> La maison m'appartient, je le ferai connaître, . . .
> (4.7.1557–58)

The knowledge that Orgon achieves so untypically is thus allied to the helplessness that the bearers of that knowledge suffered during the major action of the play. Knowledge unties no knot: it merely makes the blocked situation harder to bear:

> Ma foi, je suis confus, et n'ai pas lieu de rire.
> (4.8.1566)

If Orgon's achievement of knowledge makes us aware of how little it can do to avert catastrophe (act 5 is an act of repeated catastrophic blows) Tartuffe's bid for power brings him into direct confrontation with the real source of knowledge and power in the body politic—the king. Tartuffe's denunciation of Orgon to the king is explicable in terms of the character's malice or lust for revenge but essentially it is a step outside the boundaries of comic illusion. The logic of Tartuffe's downfall is not analogous to that of tricksters like Scapin or Volpone who overreach themselves. They are their own antagonists and spin out of control willfully. Tartuffe fails because he becomes a direct threat to the real world beyond the stage.

In lighter comedies the dramatist turns toward the real world at the end in order to include it in the celebration on stage. Here the audience is included as a witness to the threat posed by Tartuffe to each of them as citizens of an ordered society. The hypocrisy that took root in a family, reaching the court, challenges law itself. The final discovery joins knowledge with power, and the Exempt's recapitulation of the scene before the king grants effective authority to the perception we have always, though helplessly, shared with the sane people of the play.

Molière's turning to the king is not a grace note or a piece of flattery, but a necessary outcome of the serious threat posed by Tartuffe and the earlier defeats of discovery. When the clown commits acts of aggression against his audience, cursing them or acting obscenely, they can defend themselves with ridicule, for he is harmless. Tartuffe's aggression is too specifically harmful to be defeated by laughter. Molière's play ends with the admission that the art of the comic poet, or more exactly, the satirist, is only partly completed in the theater. Its fruition is in the real action taken by real people against real evil.

The ending of *Tartuffe* reminds us of the failure of the conventional devices of comedy to deal with vice too real to be judged and tamed by what are, after all, artifices. At its end this public play becomes dependent on reality to make discovery effective. In other words, because of its specific public theme, *Tartuffe* is ultimately not an independent structure as a comedy.

Le Misanthrope, a play in which the public theme is rooted in the study of a nobly eccentric mind, is a much more private and self-consistent work. Its ending arises with true neoclassical ferocity out of those insoluble conflicts of character and feeling that are clearly stated at the opening. Of Molière's major plays, it gives the least impression of movement because the basis of its major action is the repetition of a confrontation (between Alceste and Célimène) that always ends in failure.[19] If the movement of this comedy is a projection of the inner movement of the protagonist, as Copeau says,[20] then this movement can only be one of passion and its frustration countering each other into stasis. Structurally, this play is remarkably similar to the farcelike *George Dandin*. There also we have a protagonist possessed of knowledge, attempting to convince others of its truth and advancing from one failure to the next until he leaves the stage, totally isolated and defeated.[21] In that brutal play the repeated encounter between the victim and his enemies displayed the impossibility of denouement. He dreams of untying the deadlocked situation but his projects are all reversed and he is reduced to silence.

Le Misanthrope is a far more humane play, set in a high and polite milieu. Its hero is not a base victim but a violent and impassioned critic of the society around him. Yet like the farce hero he is trapped in a repeated series of actions that deny his expectations. Release for Alceste and denouement for the plot that emerges from his character can only come from one person—Célimène, the woman who can never grant him what he desires.

Thus the comparatively simple and conventionally comic structure of the repeated contretemps from which there is no issue is complicated in a way that reminds us of tragedy.[22] The trap is not, as it would be in simpler comedies, the reflection of a humor's obsession or the logic of an imposed situation, but rather the result of a collaboration between situation and character. The denial of movement is rooted in the opposing wills of Alceste and Célimène caught in a situation that they partly create and that makes it impossible for their relationship to succeed. The deadlock, of which the play is the brilliant exposition, is composed of the moral rigidity of Alceste, its opposite, the flexible and evasive coquetry of Célimène, and the fatal tie that links him to her in spite of their incompatibility.

This is the heart of the play and this is where its movement of passion neutralized by frustration is most clearly felt. All the rest of the action, Oronte's sonnet and Alceste's "case," is illustrative material. The losing of the case is an indicator of time, a turn for the worse that makes us aware in act 5 that time is running out. But these are incidents moving in the background that emphasize, by their very development, the lack of movement in the central situation: a confrontation between a man and a woman that cannot be successfully resolved.

As usual in Molière's comedies, the motif of discovery plays a major role in creating the deadlock as well as a more conventional one in bringing about the end. Discovery in the special social sense of the ruthless analysis of character is the subject of the two great "portrait" scenes that mark the early (2.4) and closing (5.4) actions of the play. The most turbulent explosion of the play is Alceste's false discovery of Célimène's "unfaithfulness" (4.3) and Alceste's very raison d'être philosophically is the ideal of sincerity, the exposure of truth in all social relationships:

> Je veux que l'on soit homme, et qu'en toute recontre
> Le fond de notre coeur dans nos discours se montre,
> Que ce soit lui qui parle, et que nos sentiments
> Ne se masquent jamais sous de vains compliments.
>
> (1.1.69–72)

The target of discovery is also the one that Alceste sets himself in his series of encounters with Célimène. The persistent refrain of "vous vous expliquerez," "vous vous déclarerez," "vous prendrez parti," (2.4 and repeated in 5.2) put the burden of discovering her heart on Célimène. This is a burden she will not accept until, herself a victim of discovery, she chooses Alceste but not the lonely life that is his condition for taking her.

Discovery is a creator of the deadlock, the insufferable situation from which Alceste wants to break away and a factor of apparent denouement in that it creates the situation which gives him his ironic release. One can demonstrate how this motif, embracing the play, contributes to its formal unity and especially to the totally rational but hardly comic necessity of the end.

Sincerity is Alceste's eccentricity. It is his fate, a noble peculiarity that has heroic and absurd aspects. His passion to expose whatever is false in society is heroic in its adherence to strict principles of truth and in its lack of self-regard, but is at the same time ridiculous in its rigidity:

> *Philinte:* Je vous dirai tout franc que cette maladie,
> Partout où vous allez, donne la comédie,
> Et qu'un si grand courroux contre les moeurs du temps
> Vous tourne en ridicule auprès de bien des gens.
>
> (1.1.105–8)

Alceste, exposer of pretense, is in Philinte's words a sick man, even a madman, and his whole enterprise foolish. Truth-telling is an impasse for Alceste because it is an uncontrollable humor and because it earns him enemies (Oronte) and blocks his success in society (the case). Alceste sees only two ways out of this trap, two possible endings to the action of which he is the protagonist. One is to escape:

> Et parfois il me prend des mouvements soudains
> De fuir dans un désert l'approche des humains.
>
> (1.1.143–44)

The other is to turn Célimène into an image of himself, a partner purified by the cleansing flame of his love:

> sans doute ma flamme
> De ces vices du temps pourra purger son âme.
>
> (1.1.233–34)

Célimène, however, is Alceste's opposite. To his passion for discrimination she opposes a lively social tact that entertains fools. To his angry discovery of truth, no matter what the cost, she opposes the exploitation of discovery as a social game of denigration with no moral base whatsoever. Alceste's angry interruption of Célimène's series of satiric portraits of people in society (2.4) is based on the difference between his self-wounding, isolating moral anger and her brilliant and popular performance. He blames her audience for encouraging her irresponsibly sharp tongue:

> Non, morbleu! c'est à vous; et vos ris complaisants
> Tirent de son esprit tous ces traits médisants.

Son humeur satirique est sans cesse nourrie
Par le coupable encens de votre flatterie; . . .

(2.4.659–62)

But his objections founder on the dangerous points that Célimène's
exposures of social folly are no different from his own, and that his
criticism of the conversation is simply perverse. Alceste is thus defeated on two major issues in his first confrontation with Célimène. His
plan to force her to choose between him and his foppish rivals—in
other words, to discover herself "Ou pour eux, ou pour moi, faire
expliquèr votre âme," (2.4.562)—is foiled by the arrival of the babbling
crowd. Then his attempt to stop the chatter of denigration is rejected as
hypocritical. Discovery is both defeated and robbed of its moral
significance. Célimène will not expose herself to him and instead displays a cheapened version of his satire against man. The trap in which
Alceste finds himself is summed up in a ridiculous gesture of immobility at the end of 2.4. The aristocratic fools, his rivals, decide to stay in
Célimène's salon and Alceste, jealous of their presence, is forced to
ape them:

Sortez quand vous voudrez, Messieurs; mais j'avertis
Que je ne sors qu'après que vous serez sortis.

(2.4.735–36)

Only the summons from the marshals of France themselves get him off
the stage, promising to return and close the debate.

In the sequence of scenes from Alceste's entrance into Célimène's
salon until his departure, Molière displays with great clarity the failure
that is at the heart of this play. Rooted in the logic of Alceste's character and in the fate that made him fall in love with Célimène, this failure
is the man's inability to make her discriminate as he, endangering
himself, discriminates between truth and pretense. Célimène, in choosing him, would hypothetically bring the play to a happy end by crowning Alceste's project with success. Molière, in his ending, makes her
do just this at the last moment, showing that failure is a necessary
result of what the characters are. No action of which they are capable
can release them from it.

The three scenes that end the play (5.2 to 5.4) repeat and intensify all
the material of the sequence discussed above. They end the play entirely within its own terms, as repetition, without any interference by
external factors and without the addition of any new material. The
changes in the background plot—the loss of Alceste's case—only add
urgency to the very situation with which the action between the pro-

tagonists opens. Alceste, who already at the beginning of the play contemplated escape, is now closer to taking the step:

> Allons, c'est trop souffrir les chagrins qu'on nous forge:
> Tirons-nous de ce bois et de ce coupe-gorge.
>
> (5.1.1521–22)

Now this project of escape directly involves Célimène. He wants her to choose not only himself but his rejection of society:

> Il faut qu'elle consente au dessein qui m'amène; . . .
>
> (5.1.1578)

Thus at the beginning of 5.2, Alceste, driven into a corner by the eccentricity that isolates him and makes him savor the wounds of injustice rather than fight those who inflict them, is as dependent as he was at the opening of the play on Célimène's choosing him. Célimène, as always, is the figure of release. Her decision alone can apparently change the tenor of the action. The last sequence of scenes, by its repetition of the earlier sequence, shows why this change is impossible. Célimène is the trapped figure in these last stages of the play. Apparently in the same situation as she was at the beginning, a manipulator of the social game, a witty critic and exposer of others, but secretive and defensive of her own privacy, she is now reversed. The social game turns against her. It is she who is manipulated and exposed. Her privacy is assaulted, and her freedom of not choosing is taken away from her.

The sequence opens with a repetition, partly a parody, of Alceste's earlier demand that Célimène choose. His nagging earlier on "Aujourd'hui vous vous expliquerez," (2.4.563) turns here into the double assault of Alceste and Oronte both pressing her to choose. Célimène is being asked to reveal herself and lose the freedom of her social mask. Her speech, they demand, must be unambiguous:

> *Oronte:* Je ne veux qu'un seul mot pour finir nos débats.
>
> (5.3.1667)

Even her silence will be no refuge:

> *Alceste:* Et moi, je vous entends si vous ne parlez pas.
>
> (5.3.1668)

Célimène, defending herself, tries to draw a distinction between the

secret choice of the heart and public commitment, which is a discovery
of that choice. She is not prepared to speak out:

> Je trouve que ces mots qui sont désobligeants
> Ne se doivent point dire en présence des gens; . . .
>
> (5.2.1631–32)

But the developing situation is moving inevitably towards discovery.
The entry of the crowd (5.3 and 4), which in the earlier sequence
interrupted Alceste's attack, here intensifies the pressure on Célimène.
Éliante is for discovery:

> Et je suis pour les gens qui disent leur pensée.
>
> (5.3.1662)

and the hostile group that gathers around Célimène in the final scene
gathers expressly for a ceremony of exposure.

The full stage at the beginning of this scene is an ironic fulfillment of
Célimène's desire for company, which so angered Alceste earlier because of its lack of discrimination:

> La peur de leur départ occupe fort votre âme.
>
> (2.4.734)

It is ironic because the game of discovery is now played against her. Its
logic is displayed in the series of exits that follows the revelations of
her letters, leaving Alceste and Célimène facing each other on a stage
that can never again be full. The closing sequence is thus the opposite
of the earlier one in terms of its movement. The earlier group of scenes
begins with the confrontation between Alceste and Célimène that is
interrupted by the crowd, continues with the false discoveries of the
"portraits," and ends with Alceste leaving a scene still peopled by
Célimène and the fops. The closing sequence begins with Oronte and
Alceste confronting Célimène, the crowd gathers to intensify the confrontation by exposing Célimène's game, their exits gradually empty
the stage, which now directs all attention to the space between Alceste
and Célimène. This is the play's climactic moment of choice and failure, and the exits that follow from it, first Célimène's and then Alceste's, leave a void that the happy survival of the raisonneur
spectators—Philinte and Éliante—cannot dispel.

The formal discoveries in this scene are parallel in tone to those of
2.4 but totally different in their consequences. The earlier character
sketches were displays of Célimène's wit, and the rejection of Al-

ceste's interruption suggested that her game could go on. These later character sketches are products of the same wit, but they end the game by revealing its deceitfulness. The exposing of people behind their backs, once a joke, becomes an exposure of the witty talker when the victims are her audience:

> *Clitandre:* . . . nous allons l'un et l'autre en tous lieux
> Montrer de *votre* coeur le portrait glorieux.
> (5.4.1693–94, my emphasis)

Here again Célimène is the opposite of Alceste, although she imitates his critical style. His openness reveals pretense to its face so he can never be exposed, only ridiculed or hated. Her criticism is a strategy for avoiding true discrimination. It reveals nothing but her own falseness, the adaptation of her opinions to whoever is her partner in conversation. Revelation thus traps her by exposing her secret:

> *Oronte:* Vous me faites un bien, me faisant vous connaître.
> (5.4.1704)

Discovery acts like a natural disaster in this play, sweeping away all the peripheral characters and leaving the two survivors and their confidants amidst the ruins. This is ironically the single moment of success for Alceste. Célimène, exposed and deserted, speaks plainly:

> J'ai tort, je le confesse, . . .
> (5.4.1739)

She admits that he is justified, even in his extreme criticism of her behavior:

> Vous en êtes en droit, lorsque vous vous plaindrez,
> Et de me reprocher tout ce que vous voudrez, . . .
> (5.4.1737–38)

It is a moment of possible change, the single moment in the play that suggests even the possibility of a release from the knot of the stalled relationship. Célimène has changed, but Alceste, of whom Donneau de Visé says in the *Lettre écrite sur la comédie du Misanthrope,* "on peut dire qu'il soutient son caractère jusques au bout,"[23] meets her change with the full rigor of his unbending consistent demand. He has not been exposed and his unexhausted humor can seek no other end than the one that he has been rehearsing in each encounter since the opening of the play.

No interruption is needed to break the flow of this final confrontation. Neither Célimène's revelation of herself nor her willingness to accept marriage can untie the knot or alter the inevitable progress of Alceste into isolation. The last words of the play are an ironic comment on the frustrated action that has characterized his entire career. Philinte, his friend, proposes foiling Alceste's culminating and most logical decision to leave the social world:

> *Philinte:* Allons, Madame, allons employer toute chose,
> Pour rompre le dessein que son coeur se propose.
> (5.4.1807–8)

Related to farce on the one hand by its repetition of scenes of contretemps, *Le Misanthrope* is related to neoclassical tragedy on the other by its spare arrangement of those factors of character and situation that make a certain end inevitable. The structure of repetition is the simplest way of displaying a usually ridiculous necessity like that of Dandin's cuckoldry. Its logic in farce is the linear logic of intensification; one thing is like another, but worse. In *Le Misanthrope* it is the *contrast* between the two great scenes of discovery that demonstrates the necessity of Alceste's failure and the impossibility of release. This contrast emphasizes the difference between Célimène's victory and her defeat, between the rejection of Alceste's criticism and its justification, and between the full stage and the empty stage.[24] The impossibility of turning this reversal into a happy end is the true proof of the unusual rigor of this play's structure. Célimène's choice has been Alceste's aim for five acts. But when it comes it only makes more clear why his victory is indistinguishable from defeat. The unexpected act brought about by drastic reversal and discovery returns us to the expected impasse. The consistency of a pattern is rarely so complete in high comedy, and never elsewhere so expressive of defeat.

But Molière was capable of imagining a more gentle, ironic consistency that allows for the impossibility of change in a humor but devises a way out in keeping with the madness that it attempts to harness. It is no accident that the way out both in *Le Bourgeois gentilhomme* and *Le Malade imaginaire* is through play-acting. In both plays "theater" and a troupe of professional actors are brought on to create the make-believe world in which reasonable people consciously adjust themselves to the fantasies of the madman in order to achieve the happy ending:

> *Covielle:* Ne voyez-vous pas bien que tout ceci n'est fait que pour

nous ajuster aux visions de votre mari, que nous l'abusons
sous ce déguisement, . . .
(*Le Bourgeois gentilhomme,* 5.6)

Le Malade imaginaire is the more humane example of the success of
the carnivalesque happy end because the device of the theater is linked
to a process of recognition. In this comedy the happy ending is made
possible by the collaboration of common sense with its antagonist—
obsession. The play depends for its benign outcome on the obsessed
character's achieving a limited recognition reached in steps, like the
stages of a geometrical proof, a recognition that, however, does not
violate the logic of his mania. So Argan holds the stage in the great
ceremony of the final tableau in the impregnable classic position of the
fool at one with his folly. As Béralde says, it is a carnival, and as a
parody of medical jargon, it aptly crowns the play's satire, but the
carnival king imposes his fantasy on all the participants who are not
mocking him but adapting themselves to his hallucinations:

Angélique: Mais mon oncle, il me semble que vous vous jouez un
peu beaucoup de mon père.
Béralde: Mais, ma nièce, ce n'est pas tant le jouer que s'accom-
moder à ses fantaisies.

(3.14)

Instead of purging the folly the ceremony allows it to continue even to
defeat death:

Vivat, vivat, vivat, vivat, cent fois vivat,
Novus Doctor, qui tam bene parlat!
Mille, mille annis et manget et bibat,
Et seignet, et tuat!

(Troisième intermède)

Yet Argan achieves a kind of recognition, which comes to him in three
stages, in the form of three didactic playlets casting him in his favorite
roles of sick man and dead man. Stage-managed by the resourceful
Toinette, the playlets are trials of medicine, the false wife, and the true
daughter. In each trial Argan sits as judge, though himself an interested
party, and in each case the defendant presents himself in a way that
modifies or breaks Argan's obsession. As with the repeated situations
in *Volpone,* these playlets reenact the obsessive scene only to destroy
it. Thus the farcical medicine practiced by the mock doctor Toinette
produces Argan's strongest glimmer of awareness that doctors may be
dangerous. Her offhand advice that he get rid of an eye and a hand for

his own good breaks through to the source of common sense and self-preservation still in him:

> Me couper un bras, et me crever un oeil, afin que l'autre se porte mieux? J'aime bien mieux qu'il ne se porte pas si bien! La belle opération, de me rendre borgne et manchot!
>
> (3.10)

Argan is still the victim of "l'entêtement de la médecine." He does not see through Toinette's brazen parody, but her outrageousness uncovers the one weak link in the armor of his folly. Argan's animal self-love, which the quacks have exploited for their own good, now performs its true office of self-defense. The two didactic playlets that follow deal with Argan's other obsession, his wife's and his daughter's future. The scene of death is a scene that has been imagined and even enacted before in the play. It is the subject of a discussion with the lawyer and Béline about Argan's will (1.7), and little Louison plays dead as a way of getting Argan to stop beating her (2.7). The motif of death is central to the play, as Gide pointed out in his *Journals:*

> And what solemnity, what a *schaudern,* each scene receives from the secret contact with death. It is with death that everything sports; it is made a sport of; it is made to enter the dance.[25]

Here counterfeit death is the perfect agent of recognition for the man who undergoes it with some trepidation:

> N'y a-t-il point quelque danger à contrefaire le mort?
>
> (3.11)

A logical extension of his obsession, it nevertheless enlightens him as to the true nature of his wife and the loyalty of his daughter. The farcical structure of the trick and the didactic obviousness of the juxtaposition create a situation broad and unambiguous enough even to penetrate Argan's fog. His resurrection gives us not a new man but one who has been made to bear a certain amount of reality. Thus, the Argan who puts on the faculty robes and swears *Juro* at the climactic points of the ceremony remains an unexhausted humor, the only still point in the burlesque around him. At this point those two opposites, recognition and obsession, meet to bring about the play's ironic happy end.

The carnival at the end of this play is an unusually tolerant one in Molière's work. The tableau includes everyone—lovers, servants, reasonable men, actors and the presiding fool. Unlike his predecessor,

Sganarelle in *L'Amour médecin,* Argan is not trapped by the festive concluding ballet.[26] It is not a device to trick him while his daughter runs away with her lover. It is as genuine an image of comedy as a healing art as Molière could devise. The participants will enjoy it, as Béralde says:

> Nous y pouvons aussi prendre chacun un personnage, et nous don-ner ainsi la comédie les uns aux autres. Le carnaval autorise cela.
>
> (3.14)

It is delightful as well as useful.

This gently ironic civilizing of the deadlock of obsession is as far as Molière can go towards dramatizing change. Like Jonson in *Bartholomew Fair* he uses an image of carnival to enable him to make his ending truly genial and inclusive of all but the villainous doctors. Jonson's carnival is real; it existed outside the theater. Molière's is supremely artificial but these carnivals save both somber comic artists from the consequences of comic creeds that feed on trickery and obsession but find change unbelievable.

5

Patterns of Resolution in Shakespeare's Comedies

> *release me from my bands* . . .
> —*The Tempest*

Recognitions in Jonson's and Molière's comedy are abrupt and stunning. The revelation in *Volpone* is destructive, it is a silencing coup in *L'École des femmes,* and an astounding trick in *Epicoene.* Comedies of obsession, plays in which humor characters occupy the stage, do not commonly end in ways that modulate the impasse or turn it into something new. Overdo's discovery of his human frailty is uncharacteristic of Jonsonian endings; much more characteristic is Busy's absurd conversion to silence by a puppet. Overdo's discovery is an image of credible change, a transformation of ignorance into knowledge, and what is more, knowledge that does not destroy. Discovery and the knowledge it brings is usually destructive in satirical comedy of the humor who can only survive, albeit ironically, if the world adapts itself to his madness. That is why the masquerade at the end of *Le Malade imaginaire* is such a powerful and suggestive image of one kind of comic ending. It is as far as Molière can go in dramatizing transformation. Argan's passage from patient to doctor is a contrivance of comic art. It uses actors and masks to bluff an absurd change. The device is transparent but its consequences are humane. Obsession and playful spectacle meet to make resolution possible with the minimal presence of recognition.

Shakespeare's comedies make it possible for us to believe in change as an element of resolution. Indeed, this often becomes a matter of faith, and this emphasis on the reality of change involves a more patient exploitation of recognition. Change in Shakespearean comedy has two faces.[1] One is the aspect of instability, the tangle of errors produced by passion, disguise, interchangeable twins, accident, and malice. The other is the aspect of revelatory change that puts an end to error and instability and implies their transformation into truth and stability. The movement from one to the other is the characteristic movement of Shakespeare's romantic comedy. We find it in the earliest play, *The Comedy of Errors,* in which protean change of shape or loss of identity is a nightmare until recognition restates and reconstitutes identities in terms of the family group, and we find it in the great final romances, in which transformation is both magic and real.

Change at the end of Shakespeare's comedy is rarely absurd or totally ironic. The most extreme changes, like those of the lovers in *A Midsummer Night's Dream* who move from a state of impasse to one of resolution, are not merely the consequences of devices and benevolent trickery but are thought of by those who undergo them as something of a mystery. The height of deadlock and the height of riot coincide in the violent chase through the forest, but though the change from that hysteria is swift, the lovers' awakening is felt to have a meaning. It is reflected upon by all the major characters, including Bottom. And Puck in his epilogue suggests to the spectators that they also have had a part in it. The display of artifice is the theatrical expression of an inner movement of the imagination (a dream) shared by the central characters and the audience.

The upward swing in Shakespearean comedy, the change out of error and confusion, may be the work of apparent accident as in *The Comedy of Errors* or the result of guiding intelligence as in *The Tempest*. It may be the result of a victory over malice and evil intent as in the problem plays, or over the kinds of impasse caused by bad luck and the lack of self-knowledge as in *Twelfth Night*. But however artful the victory, however contrived—and often the contrivances of resolution are deliberately called to our attention as in the narrated recognitions and the transformation scene of *The Winter's Tale*—it asks for our assent with a minimum of irony. This is because in the simplest as well as in the most complex plays, in those that involve evil as well as in those that only combat misunderstanding, the progress toward ending is felt to be also a progress (sometimes problematic and flawed, as in the case of Bertram) toward a new integration of character, a reappraisal of self in the light of discovery. This is not always as explicitly stated as it is by Gonzalo in *The Tempest* when he takes account of the wondrous losings and findings of a voyage in which the travelers all find themselves "where no man was his own." And discovery, even in *The Tempest,* is not the same as change, as Sebastian and Antonio demonstrate. But neither is discovery only a trick of comic plots. The progress toward discovery in many of the plays is a kind of a trial. In the tragi-comedies it is a trial indeed—in the course of which the truth is put together like pieces in a puzzle. The subject of most of the untying action in *Twelfth Night,* starting with Antonio's intervention (3.4), is the mistaken recognitions that prolong the deadlock even while advancing erratically toward its release. These mistakes create awareness of a solution only in Viola. Mostly they create pain and disappointment in the victims of error, but that is the way they earn their release and enlightenment. That is their trial, and its often cruel exposures echo in the laconic words spoken when it is all over:

> *Olivia:* A sister! you are she.
>
> (5.1.326)[2]

Recognition does not have to be explicitly stated as the reappraisal of a character's past for us to feel that this is what is meant by the lucid division into pairs and family groups at the end of Shakespeare's romantic comedies. The finding of a lover, a father or a mother is in most cases synonymous with the finding of self, and even if that discovery is ironic, like Benedick's, it is also the affirmation of his change in the teeth of those who would mock him. Only in a problem play like *All's Well* does the recalcitrance of a victim of error like Bertram obstinately survive the trial that should create recognition. There, as in the other tragi-comedies, the benevolent device that combats malice or lust takes precedence over change as a motif of ending. Angelo and Bertram are foiled, exposed, and pardoned. They are judged and released by the authority and grace of a benign trickster who does not so much demand recognition as submission.

Shakespeare's comic endings are more stable than those of Jonson and Molière because they include more. Their display of artifice and contrivance is not at the expense of feeling and mystery.[3] Change is never simple, but is shadowed by what is constant and unchangeable. Jaques and Malvolio state what comedy cannot resolve in endings that resolve most problems with the expected neatness. It is this unironic balance, struck between whatever ties the knot, that which creates the deadlock but does not disappear, and the newly found possibilities of release that makes Shakespeare's endings so different from those of Jonson and Molière. Orsino does not become another man; his weaknesses are present at the end as they were at the beginning. Similarly the happy lovers of *A Midsummer Night's Dream* betray no sense of déjà vu as they watch the play that reenacts their plight in the forest. In this they reveal the unbroken logic of their characters. Only rarely does comic form tolerate the kind of moralizing that would make change

explicit. Instead, we infer change from the discoveries that turn unnatural situations into natural ones, from the final vindication of what
was always secretly true but had been hidden by error, disguise, or evil
intent. What follows, then, is an attempt to analyze a few of the patterns of ending that seem characteristic of Shakespeare's art.

Shakespeare in his first encounter with the plot and characters of a
Roman comedy, *The Comedy of Errors,* proposes a new kind of shape
for the comic plot.[4] Plautus's play begins with the ironical detached
prologue of the slave, who supplies the information the audience needs
to understand the action. The absurd, accidental foundations of the
plot are made clear enough in this section. This is what we are to
expect, a familiar tall story of accidental parting and accidental reunion. The absurd happy ending is implicit in the absurd data of the start.
In other words, the change from a situation of frustration to one of
fulfillment occurs without a corresponding change in tone or mood or
without any design impressing itself on the mind.

Shakespeare's opening, on the other hand, is pathetic in tone and
creates the expectation of a catastrophic end. Both tone and expectation must turn into their opposites if a happy end is to be achieved. The
wheel, proceeding in a downward catastrophic direction, must, in a
counter movement, turn upwards again. The opening scene, then,
creates a pattern pressing towards completion that the ensuing action
does complete in a contrary yet inherently logical way.

The beginning of this play looks forward darkly to its end. A time
limit is set for the payment of the fine, that is in all probability a time
limit for the forfeit of Egeon's life:

> Yet this my comfort, when your words are done,
> My woes end likewise with the evening sun.
>
> (1.1.26–27)

In addition, Egeon's recounting of his family's woeful history makes us
aware at this early stage of a repeated pattern of separation,[5] search,
and return that links the exposition of past events with the action of the
play proper and thus adds a color of necessity or at least probability to
the discoveries of the final scene. The play then begins with a seemingly literal, but in hindsight partly symbolic, narration of a journey, a
birth, an attempted return, a catastrophic separation, a fruitless search,
and a despairing journey home again that leads us to the *now* of the
opening and the "end" of Egeon's life:

> But here must end the story of my life, . . .
>
> (1.1.137)

This trick of exposition makes of the play's beginning the end of a catastrophic cycle that the ensuing action imitates in a farcical manner, penetrates with analogical threads of seriousness, and completes happily.[6] The pathetic, slow-paced search of father for sons and brother for brother is continued as the increasingly hectic chase across the stage of the characters fleeing from or searching for each other.

> *S. Antipholus:* Why, how now, Dromio, where run'st thou so fast?
> *S. Dromio:*   Do you know me, sir? Am I Dromio? Am I your
>   man? Am I myself?
>
>   (3.2.71–74)

The narrated history of the loving family split up by the storms of fortune is acted out from a new perspective in the troubled marriage of Antipholus and Adriana, which is threatened by faithlessness. The "unjust divorce" that separated husband from wife in the storm appears in Adriana's words as the possible breakdown of the two-in-one figure of wedlock:

> . . . O, how comes it,
> That thou art then estranged from thyself?
> Thyself I call it, being strange to me,
> That, undividable incorporate,
> Am better than thy dear self's better part.
>
>   (2.2.119–23)

Such correspondences between pathetic exposition and largely farcical action give the play an inner shape that is reinforced by the time scheme and the use of place. The engineering of the end of a farcical plot like that of *The Comedy of Errors* is largely a matter of timing. The permutations of error are limited on the stage by the audience's patience and by its expectation that the climactic confrontation will finally take place after so many near misses. In the classic manner of farce the characters are made to race against the clock in a gradually shrinking space until discovery is unavoidable. Such a rhythm underlies *The Comedy of Errors*. Sunset is the critical time for two main actions: the fate of Egeon and the business of the chain. As the fatal hour approaches in act 5, the pace and violence of the action increase with the detention and escape of separate Antipholuses within seconds of each other (4.4). Similarly, the action converges on one place, the Priory. The conditions for the unavoidable confrontation are now met.

Yet the inevitability of the confrontation and the ensuing happy end is a challenge to the playwright. The whirligig can be brought to a stop at will. It is a matter of manipulating a few entrances and formulating a

series of questions and answers leading to the ones that untie the knot.
It is the obviousness of this manipulation that gives an absurd tone to
the endings of so many comedies—specifically that of Shakespeare's
Plautine source. The difference of Shakespeare's ending leads us back
to the difference of the play as a whole. One might focus this difference
by noticing an obsessive word play in the final scenes. The actions of
binding, tying, and its opposite—untying, loosening the knot, occur on
stage at the height of the frenzied action (4.4). The local brother and his
slave are bound on the advice of the quack, Pinch:

> Mistress, both man and master is possess'd:
> I know it by their pale and deadly looks.
> They must be bound and laid in some dark room.
>
> (4.4.92–94)

Then, a few moments later, the other pair rushes in, swords drawn:

> *Luciana:* God for thy mercy! they are loose again.
>
> (4.4.144)

In act 5, Egeon appears bound on his way to execution and hopes that
the chance encounter with his son will deliver him. But error foils this
recognition and it is not till the Abbess's second appearance with the
complementing twins that the real loosening gesture can be enacted:

> Whoever bound him, I will loose his bonds,
> And gain a husband by his liberty.
>
> (5.1.340–41)

Between the violent binding of one brother and the untying of the
father, the action reaches its most baffling deadlock as the detailed
recapitulations of the day's events by the different characters clash
irreconcilably:

> *Duke:* Why, what an intricate impeach is this!
> I think you all have drunk of Circe's cup.
>
> (5.1.270–71)

At this very point of deadlock, the pathetic unreciprocated recognition
of son by father also involves punning on the word *bond:*

> *Egeon:*   Is not your name, sir, call'd Antipholus?
>   And is not that your bondman, Dromio?
> *E. Dromio:* Within this hour I was his bondman, sir,

But he, I thank him, gnaw'd in two my cords:
Now am I Dromio, and his man, unbound.

(5.1.287–91)

Now this kind of punning is in the familiar manner of early Shake-speare and tying and untying (like threats of beating and torture) are the common lot of slaves and victims in Roman comedy. What makes it remarkable here is the structural use of the motif to tie together cata-strophic beginning and happy solution. In his exposition, Egeon told the Duke how the shipwrecked family tried to save itself by lashing the children to each other and to the mast only to be separated as the mast split on a rock. In the central action of the play binding and separation are the two poles of the marriage debate and they find physical expres-sion in Adriana's binding of her "possessed" husband (4.4) and in her demand that the Abbess let him go:

. . . that we may bind him fast,
And bear him home for his recovery.

(5.1.40–41)

It is on this basis that the Abbess's intervention becomes the comple-tion of a circular pattern rather than a lucky accident. Her untying of a knot of errors brings the action back to its beginning on the stage:

Why, here begins his morning story right: . . .

(5.1.357)

It complements the binding of parents and children onto the mast and at the same time demonstrates the alternative to Adriana's posses-siveness in marriage. The Abbess will "gain a husband by his *liberty*" (5.1.341), not by his bondage. Moreover, untying the knot makes possi-ble a new start, a radical return to the beginning of the whole story, the lowering of a family in the birth of twins:

Abbess: Thirty-three years have I but gone in travail
Of you, my sons, and till this present hour
My heavy burthen [ne'er] delivered.

(5.1.401–3)

The common machinery of ending in farce—the mounting rhythm of entrance and exit, the increasing violence, the shrinking space, and the racing clock—tends to produce an absurd full stop as the characters are arrested in full career, like the famous "freeze" of the entire cast of dupes at the end of *The Government Inspector*. Such a "freeze" is a stage picture of imprisonment in the confines of irreparable folly. Shakespeare's ending of circular return by linking beginning and end with a chain of metaphor and gesture reveals the benevolent moral design in seemingly chaotic events and lays the foundations for his later, more patient studies of change in comedy.

In the comparatively simple action of *The Comedy of Errors* the straightforward confrontation of central characters is enough to bring about recognition—here simply the correct identification of the characters by each other. Recognition is still difficult, as Egeon sadly finds out, not because of some moral flaw in him or in his son but because of the limitations imposed by circumstance on our perceptions. Once the conditions are there recognition follows pat. It is a knowledge that releases the characters from their mistakes without demanding that they earn their freedom by changing. Indeed, change in this play is feared by the victims of error as a Circean spell of metamorphosis turning them into what they are not. The end brings the characters back to what they were—brothers, sons of a father and a mother—perfect only in the narrow sense of the complete family unit.

Losing, seeking, and finding are also at the heart of the inner plot in *The Tempest*. Set down in a confined and bare space, the victims of shipwreck, convinced of the loss of their dear ones, move across the island in a despairing quest that is also their trial. It is their performance in this trial, not luck or chance, that determines the outcome of their quest. Alonso's recognition, after Ariel's speech, of the moral logic of his loss—"Therefore my son i'th'ooze is bedded" (3.3.100)—is a necessary antecedent to his happy confrontation with Ferdinand. And Ferdinand's withstanding the trials of physical labor and of continence before marriage earns him his right to Marina's hand:

> . . . All thy vexations
> Were but my trials of thy love, and thou
> Hast strangely stood the test.
>
> (4.1.5–7)

Like *The Comedy of Errors, The Tempest* has clearly limited boundaries of time and place for its action, thus throwing emphasis on an end that is at a determined point from the beginning and that is brought nearer by each word and gesture.[7] No locus of the theatrical imagination is more clearly outlined than the "uninhabited island" of the play, "this bare island" of Prospero's epilogue. Ephesus teems with activity, commercial and sensual, and yet it shrinks by coincidences around the twins until their paths have to cross. Prospero's island is empty, innocent of any effects of civilization but those imposed on it by its magus

or the castaways, so that the wanderings of the separate groups of the
shipwreck are plotted on a lucid moral map with every step, be it one of
temptation, of despair or of biting guilt bringing them nearer the inevitable confrontation with the author and observer of their pains.[8] After
the prologue of the storm, the play's action opens where it will end
three hours later—at Prospero's cell—the interim being a quest in
which those who have lost each other earn the right to find each other,
discovering themselves in the process.

The sea-girt boundaries of the island form one of the three gradated
spaces in which the circular plot of losing, searching, and finding is
enacted. The largest space is not seen on the stage. It is encompassed
by Naples, Milan, and Tunis; yet it embraces the real presence of the
theater audience as an extension of that space. The seeds of the drama
are planted in the Italian cities, the consequences of acts plotted there
spread to remote seas, and when the price of treachery has been paid,
the imagined action returns to those same cities when the play is over.
This imagined space is the arena in which Providence labors in its great
cycle; a moral circumnavigation follows the paths of both sin and virtue from their origins in the private character and the body politic to
their expansion across the world in characteristic acts of aggression
and sympathy and finally to their return, rewarded and chastened, to
the places where it all started. The stage action shows the interruption
of a morally meaningless return (from Tunis to Naples) and its continuation as a morally symbolic return enriched by change and repentance.

But uniquely in this play Shakespeare makes the formal completion
of the fictional pattern dependent on action in the real world. Prospero's return to imaginary Naples and Milan requires of the spectator a
gesture of release and sympathy that both imitates Prospero's good
deeds in the play and contributes human breath to the beneficial labors
of Providence. The epilogue, by repeating the crisis of confinement by
magic and release, goes beyond the elegant request for applause and,
making of the spectator not only a judge but a necessarily fallible
seeker for divine mercy himself, it exposes the end of the play to
thoughts of real judgment and real mercy. The neatness of the fictional
comic return is thus qualified by the reminder of the unfinished real
business we all have with God.

Prospero's appeal against being confined on the bare island is also
the appeal of the actor who fears the redundancy of outliving the illusion that gave him our grace and that of the victim of magic fearing
imprisonment by a spell. This space of magic confinement is the small-
est space of the play and its visible form is the magic circle drawn by
Prospero around his victims. This circle, mentioned in the elaborate

stage direction at 5.1.57—*"They all enter the circle"*—is the play's most tangible expression of the coercing power of Providence. The two larger figures of voyage and return over the sea and of separation and discovery on the isle emphasize the journey along the circumference the line "chalked forth" that encloses the space. Prospero's magic circle draws attention to the confined space *within* the compass of the line. Whereas the former figures indicate movement and choice of paths, the latter seems to prevent this, displaying the apparent trap of magic:

> . . . There stand,
> For you are spell-stopp'd.
>
> (5.1.60–61)

But this immobility is temporary. It begins to turn into its opposite as soon as it appears. The confining circle is drawn by a magus who has decided to *free* his victims and abandon his magic. The stillness of the "spell-stopp'd" Alonso marks the suspension of the "frantic gesture" that was the outward expression of a guilt-ridden mind and its replacement by natural movements growing out of reason, recognition, and understanding. At first these movements are not visible. They are suggested by the heavenly music that dissolves the charm and by the images of dawn melting the dark and flowing tide. But as soon as the newly arrayed Prospero appears, magic confinement gives way to natural embrace and normal human contact.

The purpose of the confining circle is then release ("To work mine end upon their senses" 5.1.53) and the spectacle of the victims, frozen by the spell, is encroached upon by the imagery of moving waters:

> . . . Their understanding
> Begins to swell, and the approaching tide
> Will shortly fill the reasonable [shores]
> That now lie foul and muddy.
>
> (5.1.79–82)

Change and return, then, are what the two journeys and the magic circle have in common. Confinement in the circle turns into release as Prospero's charm dissolves, just as loss becomes discovery as father and son confront each other. But the parallel is not perfect. Discovery replaces loss when a certain encounter is brought about by a chain of events. It is objective, a matter of naming names and stating relationships that have always been correct but were lately hidden by error. Traditionally in comedy the discoverer finds in another the object of his search; but the released victim of Prospero's spell steps out of the circle to find himself:

> . . . Go, release them, Ariel.
> My charms I'll break, their senses I'll restore,
> And they shall be themselves.
>
> (5.1.30–32)

Release into self is problematic because it poses acutely the question of change. Gonzalo's command that they all rejoice because among the many things found, they found themselves—"When no man was his own" (5.1.213)—implies that the return to self is like the finding of a son or a dukedom, a sign of providential grace. In his own case, the release from the spell is a return to a naturally virtuous self that has survived the vicissitudes of fortune unchanged. In the case of Alonso the return is to a self chastened and changed by the trials of the island. He could be said to have perfected himself. But the noble villains move out of the circle to reassume their unregenerate characters, changed only by the revelation of the impotence of their evil and saved from the consequences of this by Prospero's unilateral decision to forgive.

The discoveries of the end of the play maintain a careful balance between miraculous change and ironic consistency. The miracle of the changed father discovering his lost son playing chess with a "goddess" is countered by the irony of Miranda's innocent discovery of a "brave new world." The blunt Boatswain of the storm scene reappears to report the miracle as a series of inexplicable states: sleep, imprisonment, liberty, resulting in the very tangible restoration of the ship and discovery of the King. But just as the storm seems not to have harmed the "royal good and gallant ship," so the Boatswain appears to Gonzalo as proof of a base unalterable continuity:

> I prophesied, if a gallows were on land,
> This fellow could not drown.
>
> (5.1.217–18)

The same base continuity is apparent in the play's last discovery. Caliban and his companions burst in to discover a totally altered scene, crowded where it had been empty, resplendent where it had been plain. They themselves are grotesquely altered in their stolen frippery. But this tinsel exposes them even more than their degenerate character gives them away in every movement:

> Mark but the badges of these men, my lords,
> Then say if they be true.
>
> (5.1.267–68)

They come upon the scene but are discovered by it, and Prospero makes clear the necessity of the masters' responsibility for them:

> . . . Two of these fellows you
> Must know and own, this thing of darkness I
> Acknowledge mine.
>
> (5.1.274–76)

It is an acknowledgment that includes the figures of unregenerable baseness in the community of the play's end. All are thus revealed to themselves, even Stephano, who would deny his very name—"O, touch me not, I am not Stephano, but a cramp" (5.1.286)—and the two noble villains whose treachery is known but not made public by Prospero. The circle is then completed and the return effected without the transformation or the expulsion of the evil that lay at the plot's source. The deceiver has been pardoned and deprived of power but he has not been exposed, nor has he expressed his consciousness of guilt. That is why Prospero's appeal for the help of prayer is not an afterthought.

The ends of *The Comedy of Errors* and *The Tempest* are truly in their beginnings. The complications of misunderstanding in the farce are only an arabesque decorating the lucid and logical line of the development toward the scene of meeting and recognition. The shrinking of the wide Mediterranean scene of the story to the small circumscribed place of the stage action, as well as the radical narrowing down of a lifetime to the last few crucial hours, are formal indications that when time gives out and when all paths cross in one place all problems will be solved. The pieces of the puzzle are nearly all there from the beginning; the audience has quickly assembled them, anticipating with pleasure the inventiveness of the playwright in making up obstacles to prolong their delight.

A similar lucidity of design with its promise of progress toward an expected solution is seen in *The Tempest*. Here the movement of groups of isolated characters toward a crucial confrontation is delayed and varied by obstacles that are tests and controlled demonstrations of the characters' moral natures. Yet although the scene of confrontation is in both plays elaborately staged, little happens in its course that is not recapitulation. In *The Comedy of Errors* it is the clash of conflicting recapitulations that creates the deadlock solved at one stroke by the appearance of the mother. In *The Tempest* the actual confrontation subjects the characters to no further tests. The foregoing action has sufficiently displayed their possibilities and limitations and these are briefly surveyed in the final scene. Prospero renders mercy not because of what he sees and feels when he confronts his victims but because of a decision reached earlier. It is part of the formal clarity of both the early and the late play that the scene of confrontation, so well prepared for thematically, so probable as the fixed goal of movement in place and time, should take us back to the beginning. It is part of their serenity that neither errors of identity nor evil intentions give birth to acts that would make such a return difficult or ironic. In the Roman source play of *The Comedy of Errors* the stranger Menaechmus makes love to the courtesan in his brother's place. Shakespeare keeps on the proper side of the erotic possibilities of the double. The villains of *The Tempest* are allowed only to demonstrate the absurd consistency of their evil but their intentions are frozen by magic before they can translate them into acts. So the circle, though subjected to stress, is self-consistent and plausible at the price of giving almost no free play to that which is chronically unregenerate.

The more a comedy includes or even hints at unpleasantness that actually takes place, the more inflexible the transactions that make up the plot, the more weight is thrown onto the untying action and onto the confrontation scene in particular. This, then, tends to become a full-scale trial. *The Merchant of Venice, All's Well That Ends Well,* and *Measure for Measure* have none of the formal clarity or stable perspective of the two plays already discussed. Even though their plots may be formally spied upon throughout or guided in their last stages, the logic of aroused evil or lust either produces an irrevocable action or is separated from such an action by one drop of blood alone. That the irrevocable action turns out to be saving rather than destroying or that the bond is not foolproof is not evidence in these plays of a secret benevolence that hides in the very midst of disaster. Unlike our experience of *The Comedy of Errors* or *The Tempest,* we are not led by structure of plot and patterns of words to "gather the sequel by that went before." Indeed, it is the problematic relation of "sequel" to that which precedes it that limits the usefulness of the circular model of change and return and prompts the search for other ways of describing the link between end and beginning characteristic of comedies that would grapple with a freer, more effective evil.

Prospero's choice between mercy and revenge allows for two morally opposed sorts of endings. The choice of mercy makes possible the return and the completion of the circle, while the choice of revenge would mean a repetition of the initial act of destruction. The repetitive linear pattern of wrong-doing and punishment is alien to Shakespeare's unsatirical kind of comedy. But it is nevertheless present as an alternative "measure for measure" when the seriousness of the evil cause seems to warrant it. Shakespeare's tragi-comic middle way between these two poles, a way that belittles neither the gravity of the evil cause nor the labor of its defeat, makes new use of a classic comic convention to hold the final balance.

Readers of Roman comedy are familiar with the exploitation of confusion about identity for the creation of deadlock and comic upheaval. Characters ignorant of who they are hold the key to many happy endings that are held up until someone arrives to identify them. In Terence's *Woman of Andros,* for example, the revelation of Glycerium's real name and status makes possible her marriage to the young man with his father's consent. A more complicated knot is created when one character is taken for another, the result of coincidence or intrigue. Such an exchange of identity makes likely more far-reaching consequences; the wife may share her bed with the god standing in for the husband *(Amphitryon),* the angry citizen may put his own son in chains, thinking him to be a slave who has tricked him by standing in for his young master *(The Captives).* Such mistakings approach seriousness by creating situations that would be irreversible if not for some saving grace or lucky revelation at a crucial moment. In his tragicomedies Shakespeare comes as close as possible to dramatizing the irreversible consequences of such exchanges and his model for such a transaction is the substitution of one body for another in the encounter of sex.

The actions of exchange and substitution of one person for another underlie the tragi-comic climaxes of *The Merchant of Venice, All's Well That Ends Well,* and *Measure for Measure* in a special way. In the two latter plays the act upon which the ending movement depends and which it mainly judges is an act of sexual intercourse with a woman substituted for the intended partner. In the first play, the ghoulish yet sincere exchange of Antonio's body for the forfeited bond does not indeed take place but in its stead other seemingly irrevocable transactions are made that repeat in a minor key the crucial acts of the play and link them to the happy end. In all three plays the near fatality of an act of exchange epitomizes the many dualities of tragi-comic resolution. It is both absurd and nobly unselfish, an act of blind lust and of rightful consummation, a trick of comic convention and a commentary on character, irrevocable and yet a release.[9]

The law of exchange is the natural law of the commercial world of Venice where money and goods change hands and credit is extended in return for a bond that itself will turn into money on a given date. This is the natural cycle of business transactions controlled by law and custom and endangered by fortune. By agreeing to Shylock's "merry bond" Antonio symbolically undermines the impersonal practices of business, going even further than the generosity of "what's mine is yours" to the extreme emotional and spiritual commitment of "my life is yours."

The exchange of money for goods is an unending cycle, the aim of which is profit. The substitution of a body for one factor in the transaction makes the cycle stop before a potentially tragic exchange that is a grotesque parody of a business deal. Antonio's substitution of his body for the debt of 3,000 ducats is, structurally, a simpler form of the tragicomic knot than the parallel acts of Mariana and Helena. The women's act is real; they hand over their body to the lust of a predator and, losing the blood of virginity, redeem their enemy lover. Antonio exploits all the pathos of such an act:

> Repent but you that you shall lose your friend,
> And he repents not that he pays your debt;
> For if the Jew do cut but deep enough,
> I'll pay it instantly with all my heart.
>
> (4.1.278–81)

However, he does *not* have to spill his blood to redeem his friend. The loss of maidenhood, while irrevocable, avoids tragedy through marriage while the exchange of a life for a debt cannot be digested by comedy. So the crucial act does not take place in *The Merchant of Venice,* but in its stead a symbolic analogy occurs as its sequel and creates the knot that the resolution must untie. Portia, who has given everything to her chosen lover—"Myself, and what is mine, to you and yours/Is now converted" (3.2.166–67)—makes the final gift of her body dependent on the redeeming of Antonio's debt. Meanwhile the exchange of rings stands for the postponed consummating embrace. But the connection between the redemption of the debt and mutual possession in marriage is not as simple as that between Antonio's adoption of the debt and Bassanio's successful search for a bride. Antonio's forfeit of his body made possible his friend's success as a lover; Bassanio's requiting that generous act, even hypothetically, is falsely symmetrical. His oath protesting that he would give up his life, his wife, and all the world is heard with understandable irony by Portia:

> I would lose all, ay, sacrifice them all
> Here to this devil, to deliver you.
>
> (4.1.286–87)

For Bassanio is not his own man. Even his body is not his to give since it belongs to his wife, who has his ring. Any requiting of Antonio's friendship becomes a betrayal of his marriage. The two obligations are seemingly contradictory; they can be reconciled only by the trick of the substituted woman, which in all three plays is the condition for the male victim's ambiguous act of wrong-doing and redemption. An act of treachery, it turns out, may simultaneously be its opposite, just as giving away a ring may, in comic circumstances, also be giving it back:

> . . . when this ring
> Parts from this finger, then parts life from hence;
> O then be bold to say Bassanio's dead!
>
> (3.2.183–85)

Thus Bassanio, who does symbolically what Antonio is saved from doing, is saved from the consequences of his act by the double presence of the figure of the "young doctor of Rome," of Portia's claim and Antonio's, of male and female.

The Merchant of Venice is not a play that scatters indications of ending along its way. For instance, the bond between Shylock and Antonio, unlike Bertram's extreme conditions for bedding Helena, bears no hint in its own wording of its subversion. The ending movement, initiated by Portia's tying the consummation of her marriage to Antonio's release from the bond, is in fact an attempt to solve the relationship between the unilaterally self-sacrificing act of male friendship that begins the play and the mutual obligations of married love that it makes possible but that supersede it. That a difficult choice must be made is clear from Bassanio's dilemma with the ring. The play ends well by contriving a congruency between the genuine split in the man and the sacrificial doubleness of the woman, or between the man's harmless breach of faith and the woman's benevolent mischief.

In the other two plays the male wrongdoers are forced to reconcile their lust for one woman with their possession of another. Their own blind act serves both purposes and their evil intention is redeemed by its satisfactory outcome. Bassanio, whose courtesy and loyalty overcome his love vow, cannot in the one act express both friendship and love but must be made to seem an adulterer in order to earn his happy ending. Bassanio's "guilt" in the ring scene puts him in a position vis à vis Portia analogical to that of Antonio vis à vis Shylock. He too has broken a bond and deserves death (in lovers' rhetoric) or more prosaically, the horns of cuckold:

> Now, by mine honor which is yet mine own,
> I'll have that doctor for [my] bedfellow.
>
> (5.1.232–33)

Antonio's second binding points the parallel again. These repetitions are a reversal of the earlier binding and trial because the source of both "credit" and mercy is now Portia instead of Shylock.

Portia finally fills all possible positions vis à vis the hapless men: wronged wife, mysterious sweetheart, judicious advocate, source of credit and mercy. It is she who is "double" and not Bassanio, the target of her accusation. As such she can easily change places with herself, return the ring, and solve everything. But the initial, disturbing asymmetry remains. The self-sacrificing friend for whom Bassanio was prepared to forfeit wife and all is the odd man out. His second and excessive offer to bind his soul upon the forfeit for Bassanio's faith is a genuine but unserious gesture. He has no more role to play, for Portia's credit is given without forfeit and he has become a pawn in her game. Thus the liberation of Antonio also frees Bassanio from his tie to the older man and the conflicting obligations of friendship and marriage are resolved by making both men clients of Portia.

Unlike the other two darker tragi-comedies, the crucial acts of forfeit and bloodletting do not take place in *The Merchant of Venice*. Antonio does not give his body for his friend, nor does he spill his blood, as Mariana and Helena do to seal their status as wives. It is the avoidance of the serious transaction that makes the ending of this play a lighter affair. In its stead there is its artificial image in the coda of the rings, which exposes earlier choices and repeats the gesture of forfeit but only formally and without pain.

The very name *All's Well That Ends Well* points to a tension between the happy ending and the not-so-happy events that it compensates for.[10] Twice Helena must remind her partners in her project that "Though time seem so adverse and means unfit" (5.1.26), the end "is the renown" (4.4.36) and will justify the means by which it was achieved. In this play it is the patient plotting of a loving and understanding woman that turns the "abhorr'd ends" of a trifler who contrives against his own nobility into the hallowed end that he was fleeing:

> *Bertram:* A heaven on earth I have won by wooing thee. *(Exit)*
> *Diana:* For which live long to thank both heaven and me!
> You may so in the end.
>
> (4.2.66–68)

This transposition of ends (exchanging the irresponsible deflowering of a virgin for the consummation of a marriage) is the result of a redeeming act of substitution—"this deceit so lawful" (3.7.38) that converts bad into good without demanding the full price of recognition, neither at the moment of encounter nor at the end.

The crucial act of this play, the hidden encounter in Diana's bed, is morally two-faced. As a destructive act of lust it has no consequences because the lust remains a purpose, a wicked meaning, more in the head than in the deed. As a beneficent fact of consummation it does have consequences—the pregnancy of Helena and the fulfillment of the seemingly impossible conditions of Bertram's letter. But the initiator of the act, whether we stress its sinful or redeeming aspect, remains blind, unaware of his shame (act 4) as he is laconic in his acceptance of guilt in the final scene. Although this lack of awareness in Bertram has been considered a weakness by many,[11] it is in keeping with the play's insistence that man is judged by his acts rather than by his intentions and with the nature of the critical sexual encounter that makes beneficent use of the lover's silence, blindness, and ignorance.

The elaborate final scene of the play is disappointing if we expect a scene of recognition. It lacks the wonder of discovery and, as Bertram takes the center, develops into an unpleasant investigation of his pretensions and self-indulgent evasions. The shock of revelation that transfigures so many of Shakespeare's comic endings is absent. In its stead there is a curiously impersonal exposure of Bertram's guilt by stages until the crisis of incomprehension summed up by Diana's cryptic lines brings about the intervention of Helena:

> . . . he's guilty, and he is not guilty.
> He knows I am no maid, and he'll swear to't;
> I'll swear I am a maid, and he knows not.
>
> (5.3.289–91)

Helena is the meaning of Diana's riddle just as she, bearing ring and child, is the answer to the seemingly unanswerable challenge of Bertram's letter. This resolution, like the clever answer to a riddle, is primarily a matter of words and hidden logic, not feeling. The paradoxical formulations of Diana ("Dead though she be, she feels her young one kick. / So there's my riddle: one that's dead is quick," 5.3.302–3) do not, as in the romances, compress and strain into a line of verse a complete and astonishing turnabout of fortune. Rather they draw attention to the trick around which this resolution is built. It is this act that informs all the paradoxes and cryptic formulations of the play's final sequence. It is behind the elaborate and circular interrogations about the ring, and its peculiar nature helps to explain the flatness of the ending.

The encounter between awareness, total or partial, and blindness in varying degrees is fundamental to most kinds of comedy. It is the condition of the most primitive joke or trick played upon a victim, and much sophisticated, it underlies the illusions and misreadings of intention and action in the subtlest of comedies. The bed-trick is essentially a primitive practical joke with serious consequences. Blindness and

awareness, victim and hunter are set in clear and diagrammatic opposition in the neat and tendentious setup of darkness and silence in the
bed. What differentiates it from the simple practical joke is the physical
involvement of the "joker"; the woman in the sexual encounter is both
the player of a trick and the object of lust. She is an observer of her
victim and yet a participator in an act that changes her own status.
Intellectually superior because she *knows,* she is physically subject to
the man who "knows" her carnally though he does not recognize her.

The implications of sexual knowledge without recognition are not
ignored by Shakespeare. They are painfully analyzed by Helena, who
makes us feel the copresence in that moment of enjoyed passion and
abuse:

> . . . But O, strange men,
> That can such sweet use make of what they hate,
> When saucy trusting of the cozen'd thoughts
> Defiles the pitchy night; . . .
>
> (4.4.21–24)

What is unpleasant here is that this base form of knowing should be the
key to the happy end and that the protagonist/victim Bertram, having
blindly engendered it, is left by the dramatist on that level of knowledge until the curtain falls. In *A Midsummer Night's Dream* the erotic
confusions of the night produce a state of exhaustion out of which the
resolution can follow with the rhythmic logic of day following night.
The audience is left to make the connections between the madness of
the erotic chase, the recollections of the lovers, and the stability and
fruitfulness of the marriage bed. In *All's Well That Ends Well* blind lust
is not a prelude or foil to consummation but accompanies it and is
indistinguishable from it. This ironic salvation through blindness marks
Bertram for the rest of the play and severely limits his chances of
attaining any satisfactory recognition. Even his base companion and
moral parallel, Parolles, is observed in a moment of truth as he is
forced to come to terms with himself, to know himself a braggart. It is
the denial of this self-knowledge to Bertram that characterizes the final
scene of the play.

This scene seems to move in a way not intended, indeed specifically
rejected by those who would control it. In the brief prologue the King
makes it clear that the bitter past is to be forgiven and that complaints
about Bertram's behavior will be suppressed:

> We are reconcil'd, and the first view shall kill
> All repetition.
>
> (5.3.21–22)

However, repetition is just what the scene engineers. Although the past is buried by the King along with Helena the dialogue cannot move in any other direction. What directs the movement of the play to its final confrontation is not so much a knowing character as the fact of the consummation that throws up evidence (the rings), produces the riddles, and throws into ironic relief the angry ignorance of the King and the forced maneuvers of Bertram.

"All this may be good drama, but it is bad psychology," says W. W. Lawrence of the apparently unnecessary elaborateness of Shakespeare's denouement.[12] The postponement of the confrontation between Bertram and Helena seems to him unjustified by anything but the desire for a coup de théâtre of the kind that final scenes in comedy tend to provide. Dr. Johnson, on the other hand, found that Shakespeare was "hastening to the end of the play"[13] and precipitating the action. Both are in fact noticing the same thing: the denouement's apparent lack of interest in feeling and the seeming lapse into convention as the vindicated wife picks out her man again. Certainly Shakespeare's source in Painter is far more direct; the narrative simply brings Giletta to her husband's court to reveal herself and her children and repeat her story.[14] Dramatic tradition, on the other hand, demands revelation step by step. Certainly in comedies this stage-by-stage advance to the obvious recognition is a formula exploiting the laughable blindness of the personae to what is obvious to us. Yet in Shakespeare, perhaps most markedly in his last plays, the stages of the final recognition are an enactment of something less formal than moral—a process of awakening.

In *All's Well* quite clearly no awakening takes place. There is no major affirmative note at the end of this sequence that would make of its stages steps on such a lucid path. The protagonist has come to the final scene without self-knowledge, a bearer of false values and yet already saved. To succeed as an optimistic and harmonious ending, the denouement would have to bridge the gap between the blind knowledge of sex and the self-knowledge of discovery. This is structurally impossible because the intervening motif of regret or repentance is missing. As a second best, and more realistically in keeping with the play's mood and the protagonist's nature, the denouement recapitulates in detailed sequence instances of Bertram's falseness, mocking him at the very moment of revelation with his continued lack of self-knowledge:

> . . . But for this lord,
> Who hath abus'd me, as he knows himself,

> Though yet he never harm'd me, here I quit him.
> He knows himself my bed he hath defil'd, . . .
>
> (5.3.297–300)

Bertram's defenses penetrated anew by each twist in the scene are here totally down. His sin and salvation, the "mingled yarn, good and ill together" (4.3.71–72), are one: the former he chose, the latter chose him. Diana's speech juxtaposes Bertram's ignorance, his thoughts of abuse and defilement and his redeeming act of generation. Thus the King's stern words to the slippery youth turn out to have a fair meaning:

> Sir, for my thoughts, you have them ill to friend
> Till your deeds gain them; . . .
>
> (5.3.182–83)

The ignorant deed does produce the rational end, but the name and the thing are still separated and in his last speech the play's constantly deluded protagonist makes his love dependent surprisingly on more knowledge:

> If she, my liege, can make me know this clearly,
> I'll love her dearly, ever, ever dearly.
>
> (5.3.315–16)

J. L. Calderwood is right when he calls the final scene a "gloss on the bed-trick."[15] It is in fact a demonstration of its happy consequences but also a recapitulation of its irresolvable paradox of perversion and fulfillment. The substitution of one body for another in the dark makes of sin an illusion and a reality of marriage insomuch as we concentrate on the deed alone. At the end, when the characters confront each other in awareness as well as in daylight, the disturbing, unruly energy of sex is still there in Helena's speech next to the evidence that would harness it:

> O my good lord, when I was like this maid,
> I found you wondrous kind. There is your ring, . . .
>
> (5.3.309–10)

The ring does make a circular progress from Bertram and back to him and this might imply harmony like the return of the ring in *The Merchant of Venice*. But the encounter upon which this potential harmony is based is analyzed too vividly, is too alive to fit tamely into the formal solution. Bertram in being "kind" then was only being true to his baser natural instincts and no miracle has transformed them.

In *Measure for Measure* the bed-trick is used in an analogous way to foil evil and facilitate ending but the ideas that radiate from the act and are focused in it are of a different kind. In the denouement of this play is a good example of how Shakespeare clothes a stock device of comic resolution with meaning, thus linking the traditionally formal and self-sufficient end with the deepest concerns of the play.

There is a fundamental opposition in the play between two kinds of exchange. One kind is hard and unyielding; this is the meting out of punishment for crime, injury for injury, and measure for measure. This kind of exchange is potentially catastrophic because in its strictness it may entail death for the offender. The other kind of exchange tends to undermine catastrophe and strictness by exploiting the old device of substitution. Thus instead of an Angelo for a Claudio there is a Ragozine for a Claudio, and instead of a raped Isabella there is a betrothed Mariana in the bed. The comic exchanges represent the benevolent devices and exploitation of accident that resolve deadlocks and turn either/or situations into traps with an escape hatch.

The multiple substitutions of the end, therefore, need to be seen in the context of the important situations of exchange and substitution that form the backbone of the plot. Then we will understand how the device takes on some of the resonance of an idea.[16]

The opening gambit of the play is itself an act of substitution. Angelo is put in the place of the Duke. He is in fact called "substitute" (5.1.133, 140), but at the beginning the Duke puts it in the most pointed way:

> In our remove be thou at full ourself.
>
> (1.1.43)

The traditional comic use of the substitute figure is to solve problems, to fit into crucial slots and remain passive. Here at the opening of the play the substitute is encouraged to be active and independent and so the problems of mortality and mercy are created in order to be resolved at the end by an assortment of more conventional substitute figures. Angelo's taking of the Duke's place and his extreme interpretation of his authority create the kind of confrontation characteristic of the middle action of the play. The judge is placed opposite the sinner and asked whether he has ever been in his position:

> Whether you had not sometime in your life
> Err'd in this point which now you censure him,
>
> (2.1.14–15)

This figure is used with effective monosyllabic bluntness by Isabella:

If he had been as you, and you as he.
You would have slipp'd like him, but he, like you,
Would not have been so stern.

(2.2.64–66)

These hypothetical changes of place are of course hints of the great reversal to come when Angelo does become as Claudio. Thus far, then, the Duke's temporary abdication has created a situation in which it has become possible for characters to speculate radically on the artificiality of the separation between judge and offender and reverse them in their minds.

If change of place creates the situation and the possible exchange of moral opposites complicates it, the more conventional exchange of a woman's body for a proffered favor creates the dilemma that only the bed-trick can untie. This time Isabella and not Angelo is at the center and the suggested transaction is the substitution of her virginity for her brother's redemption, or the payment of her virginity to redeem his forfeited life. The similarity of temper that critics have often noted about Isabella and Angelo[17] is reinforced by our understanding of the formal similarity of their positions vis à vis the offender. The precise Angelo will not put himself in the criminal's place to save him though he later finds himself imitating his crime. The chaste Isabella will not put her body in the criminal's place (Angelo's power) to save him though she later finds someone else to imitate her there. She certainly has strong arguments to support her refusal but it still looks selfish in the light of the most powerful, if only evoked, substitution of this central part of the play. For it is surely Christ's sacrifice of himself, the placing of his body in the grip of death, that saved all the souls that were forfeit once to the law that doomed them as sinners. The remedy is mercy but it is brought to man by Christ's yielding himself up to save his brother. This is the unequal exchange that is the antithesis of tit for tat and measure for measure. It is a godly privilege or a martyr's. Its absoluteness cannot fit into the natural human world of comedy where the substitutions and exchanges that now begin as the action reaches its crisis are the familiar tricks played by the virtuous to beat evil at its own game.

One can judge Shakespeare's awareness of the conventionality of the device and his turning that artifice to advantage in the incident of the substitute head. Angelo's wickedness is combated by two tricks of substitution: Mariana in Isabella's place and somebody's head instead of Claudio's. But in the latter case the traditionally passive decoy of such situations, Barnardine, rebels against his role:

> I swear I will not die to-day for any man's persuasion.
>
> (4.3.59–60)

And so the hard-pressed politicians of virtue have to make use of a timely casualty to supply the deputy Angelo with the deputy (Ragozine) of a deputy head (Barnardine). The human conflict with the convention (Barnardine's refusal) makes the lucky chance more plausible and more serious.

The discovery scene in all three tragi-comedies is a judicial probe into the past, using a triallike procedure to follow closely the evasions and lies of the offender until he is brought face-to-face with the redeeming consequences of his crime. In *The Merchant of Venice* the trial of the rings is lighthearted, a joke with certain serious connections to Bassanio's dilemma; in *All's Well* the trial explores the disturbing mystery of blind knowledge in sex. In *Measure for Measure,* the longest and most elaborate of them, the trial juxtaposes the disguise of Angelo and the pretenses of Isabella and the Duke in a complex recapitulation, the formal purpose of which is to create a deadlock composed of the accumulation of frustrated endings that reveal Angelo's guilt and compromise him but depend on the "coup" of the Duke's intervention for release into action.

The awareness of the criminal is the most important structural datum of this scene.[18] Unlike Bertram and despite the limited number of speeches he is given in the scene, Angelo's conscience is awake, we know, and the encounter is therefore a subtler one than that of *All's Well*. The protagonists are more of a match for each other. Because of this the scene is also less ceremonious, less formal and more chaotic. The Duke's plan to proceed with Angelo "By cold gradation and weal-balanc'd form" (4.3.100) is hardly carried out, for a ceremony is less personal and more distanced than the passionate play-acting of this final scene.

The two major confrontations with Isabella and with Mariana reenact in a distorting glass Angelo's two critical moments—his temptation and his fall. The temptation is replayed according to Angelo's version of its consequences:

> Who will believe thee, Isabel?
>
> (2.4.154)

Isabella's denunciation, part true and part play-acting, brings out the secret only to delay revelation. The Duke's ironic rejection of her charges—

> . . . it imports no reason
> That with such vehemency he should pursue
> Faults proper to himself.
>
> (5.1.108–10)

—and Mariana's contradicting them create the deadlock and frustration needed if the "coup" of the Duke's unmasking is to work. The power of the true ending depends on the energy stalled by the false endings. Thus Mariana's unveiling, a formal gesture accompanied by formal language—

> This is that face, thou cruel Angelo,
> Which once thou swor'st was worth the looking on;
> This is the hand which, with a vow'd contract,
> Was fast belock'd in thine; . . .
>
> (5.1.207–10)

—is lost in Lucio's joke and in Angelo's evasive speech. The deadlock of frustrated endings comes to a head in the exit of the Duke and the appearance of the mysterious Friar. Here is the central situation of the play in one picture—the Duke absent, the despair of the suppliants, the impossibility of convincing the public that the judge is the villain. Thus in one scene the Duke has again set up the essence of the action: his absence and return. But this time his return is violent, a turnabout to stop all further change:

> Thou art the first knave that e'er mad'st a duke.
>
> (5.1.356)

Then the gesture of unseating Angelo completes the return:

> We'll borrow a place of him.—Sir, by your leave.
>
> (5.1.362)

The Duke's unmasking and assumption of his rightful place as ruler and judge expose the foregoing action as a trial lacking only a sentence to bring it to completion. This is the point in the play where the given facts of source material and comic convention put the most strain on artistic logic. Basically the reprieve of Angelo and the revelation of the substituted head are the facts of plot that do away with the tragic knot and replace it with a comic finale. But they are not transparent or isolated tricks. They depend on Isabella's intervention, a moment of real and difficult choice that, formally, counters the strictest exchange proposed by the Duke ("An Angelo for Claudio, death for death!" 5.1.409) with the hypothesis, secretly true, which would make that exchange unnecessary:

> Look, if it please you, on this man condemn'd
> As if my brother liv'd.
>
> (5.1.444–45)

Isabella, by kneeling for Angelo's life, puts herself in Mariana's place—"Sweet Isabel, take my part"—thus making up for her inability to put herself in her brother's place earlier in the play, and rewarding Mariana for taking Isabel's part in the bed.

The revelation of the last benefactor of cunning exchange—Claudio—puts the seal on the device and links it clearly with the tragicomic ethos. The stern resolution of "like doth quit like" is commuted to the comic solution of "Well, Angelo, your evil quits you well." (5.1.496). The balancing mutual cancellation of the former contrasts with the imbalance of evil producing good. This has happened thanks to the device of substitution, which draws the sting of both lust and murder by having them spend their force on the wrong object.

The substitutions and exchanges that in farce would be the consequence of accident and luck determined by polished geometries of plot are here both a cunning tactic to test and combat evil on the level of plot and, on a symbolic level, represent the alternative to the lex talionis, which would only exchange blood for blood. "Like quits like" is based on a primitive equation of injuries; the other exchanges produce good out of evil, no equation this time but a form of change.

Although we do not hear Isabella's assent to the Duke's offer of marriage, there is more than conventional propriety in his proposal. The self-surrender and mingling of flesh in the sacrament of marriage is the closest a Christian can come, in the natural world of comedy, to transcending self. "What's mine is yours, and what is yours is mine." (5.1.537) is the fairest and most hopeful proposal of exchange in a play whose title posits an exchange as severe as it is irrevocable.

The scenes of discovery we have discussed all lead us to contemplate the past, whether that be the past just enacted on the stage or the remoter past of the story's beginning. If the comedies of circular journey go back to the beginning, the tragi-comedies end with a scene of trial whose purpose it is to expose in a cunning and roundabout way the misdeeds that dominated the middle action and created the crisis. Such final scenes dramatize the serious principle that acts have inevitable consequences, which is modified by the comic principle that there is a device to counter every evil intent.

The happy ending of forgiveness comes when the shameful actions of the past have been reconstructed in full and in public. It is an extreme juxtaposition and puts an enormous strain on our expectations of the sinning characters who straddle contrary experiences of exposure and release without undergoing a process of conversion. Thus they remain what they always were, cast clearly against the background of their recapitulated misdeeds, but released by a duality in the misdeed itself and the generosity of others.[19] This is one of the most important significances of the conventions of recapitulation and return at the end of these plays. They enable the dramatist not just to explain the intricacies of the knot or complete a formal pattern, but to entertain the mind of his audience with the conflicting claims of happy change and ironic consistency. The new beginning that the end of comedy so often proposes cannot be really new. In the case of tragedy, death or disaster clear the scene for a fresh start, symbolized by the accession to power of a new king. In these comedies the survival of all the characters begs the question that the recapitulation and the figure of return make more specific. How much weight do we give the fiction of change, based as it is on such unpromising material?

The romantic love comedies approach their endings with a less specific focus on the past than do the tragi-comedies. Indeed, we might expect them to ignore the past altogether and instead emphasize the happy future. But the tension between consistency and change is present in all Shakespearean comedy, and, as the lovers in the plays of masking and error approach the happy end, they are made to see the growth of resolution out of the errors of the past, or the clash between the two. The characters of *Twelfth Night,* approaching the end, struggle with the puzzle of appearances as they try to make rational sense of their past encounters. In *Much Ado* Claudio's acceptance of the masked lady in marriage repeats and reverses the essential mistake of the play. Only in *As You Like It,* the least complicated play of the group, does the act of unmasking break the deadlock without reference to the past. This is because Rosalind does not have to struggle towards recognition. She can cut the knot whenever she has had enough of her game.

Unmasking is the culminating act of *Much Ado* and *As You Like It* and it is through an investigation of how unmasking is exploited and reached in both plays that one may characterize their endings. In *Twelfth Night* the leading motif of ending is properly recognition and we may therefore consider it in conjunction with the miraculous recognitions of *The Winter's Tale.*

Unmasking as a comic device is pregnant with ending because once the mask is off, the character who wore it is used up dramatically. The tensions resolved that made him interesting and complicated the plot,

he exits into the future, suddenly simpler and therefore a fitting participant in the expected solution. The suddenness of unmasking in a coup
de théâtre may give it the aura of a metamorphosis or almost miraculous change from one kind to another, from boy to girl or from death to
life. In the final scene of *As You Like It,* Rosalind appears, dazzling and
transformed, and even Hero, given the deliberate prosaic limitation of
Much Ado, reveals herself with a flourish and a hint at miracle. On the
other hand, the avoidance of the physical gesture of unmasking in
Twelfth Night questions change and introduces an element of suspension, of something unresolved, into the expected symmetry.

At its simplest, unmasking is synonymous with change and resolution, at its most complex it remains too involved with the past to signify
an unambiguous change. Each comedy takes its masks off in a different
way. Masking is both a leitmotif of *Much Ado about Nothing,* being
the condition of many of the major scenes, and the symbolic expression of the kind of society the play portrays. Near the beginning of the
play the masked dance provides the opportunity for the complication
of the intrigue and near the end the unmasking of the ladies is the signal
for its close.

But what kind of closing gesture is unmasking in the context of the
play's array of masquerades? Does the ending say anything about the
convention itself?

Much Ado is wholeheartedly a social comedy. Society is its field, a
deliberately limited area in which there is no place for the kind of
philosophical or metaphysical questions that cannot be dealt with in
the mannered discourse of witty and fashionable people. In such a
society the usual crucial distinction between true and false is not obviously more important than that between social approval and disapproval or as demanding as that between what is fashionable and
unfashionable. The sophisticates who move in such a society fear the
scorn and ridicule of their peers more than sin, and such scorn finds its
most common target in the one whose actions give him away by being
too natural. The mask is as necessary as clothing because plain-
speaking sincerity is as embarrassing as nakedness—and, moreover,
not witty. Unmasking, then, may not be as final an act here as it would
be in comedy with a more moral and critical bias. In the latter case the
mask removed reveals the truth, and in the former the cover of the
mask is often only a way of expressing the cover of any witty and
urbane attitude that is neither true nor false and cannot disappear with
the flourish of a dropped disguise.

The crisis of *Much Ado,* the scene of false accusation in church (4.1),
is disturbing because it suddenly exploits the traditional moral criticism

of masking as Hero's "cunning sin" covering itself in a "show of truth."
This is not only a gross mistake on the part of Claudio and Don Pedro,
but a style of talk and behavior foreign to the society of the play. This is
made clear for the audience by Benedick's puzzled failure to grasp the
tone of Claudio's first general words of accusation:

> *Claudio:*   O, what men dare do! What men may do! What men daily
>   do, not knowing what they do!
> *Benedick:* How now! interjections? Why then, some be of laughing,
>   as, ah, ha, he!
>
> (4.1.19–22)

This clash of tones is characteristic of the play and familiar to us
from earlier encounters, such as the mockery of Claudio's sadness in
2.1. There, Claudio's quick despair over Don Pedro's "wooing" of
Hero is encountered by Benedick's joke about fashionable poses of
mourning and melancholy:

> What fashion will you wear the garland of? about your neck, like an
> usurer's chain? or under your arm, like a lieutenant's scarf?
>
> (2.1.188–90)

To the unaffected observer the lover's melancholy is one of many
possible poses, a subject for wit. But there, unlike the church scene,
the young man's misery is soon revealed as unreal, based on misunderstanding. Prompted by the gratuitous malice of Don John, Claudio
misreads the meaning of his aristocratic friend's mask and attributes a
treacherous purpose to its harmless artificiality.

It is the harmless and playful pretense of masking, symbolized by the
formal sets of dialogue during the dance (2.1), that is the play's benevolent plot device. It has no moral or metaphysical connotations in its
context, and the victories and defeats that it engenders are those of
pride and vanity, though it does pave the way to confessions of love.
Masking of this kind is always at a tangent to feeling, apparently its
artificial opposite and exploiting it as food for wit, but secretly nour-
ished by feeling and engaged with it.

But the knot that the ending action has to untie is not created by
harmless pretenses and the wit they provoke. It is created by the
intervention of an evil nature whose flat reality is at odds with the witty
environment of the play:

> *Don John:* I cannot hide what I am: I must be sad when I have
>   cause, and smile at no man's jests; . . .
>
> (1.3.13–14)

Don John is paradoxically less of a masker than his victims. He is what he seems to be: tart, melancholy, taciturn, and an opponent of wit in his refusal to talk. In Beatrice's words, he "is too like an image and says nothing" (2.1.8), while Benedick, his opposite, is "too like my lady's eldest son, evermore tattling" (2.1.9–10).

The crisis Don John brings about draws our attention to the limitations of wit in a play that devotes so much time to its exhibition. In one scene (3.2) Don Pedro and Claudio are shown to be masters of teasing and light mockery as they exploit Benedick's change, and at the same time, extremely gullible victims of Don John's trap. The connection between the two tones, the witty and the serious, is more than that of simple contrast. The entry of real evil into the social world of practice and pretense reveals the easy surrender of wit to its opposite, a blatant impolite righteousness.

The scene that defines the problem that the denouement has to solve is the scene of false accusation in the mock wedding ceremony. Structurally, it is the crisis scene of the play in that it brings the malicious intrigue to its peak and creates an apparent ending, secretly opened up already by Dogberry and the watch, but for all the major characters, a genuine and revealing moment of choice. What each chooses to do in this scene labels him clearly as he approaches the real end. Don Pedro and Claudio falsely discover Hero's sin, while Beatrice and Benedick truly discover each other. The crisis in the plot coincides with the thematic crisis because we are led to distinguish between two moments of unmasking and discovery in the scene. The unmasking that dominates the scene is the grossest of errors, while the subtler one that follows between Beatrice and Benedick is genuine. In terms of plot, knowledge of Dogberry's success sharpens our perception of the falseness of Claudio's attack: "Out on thee seeming! I will write against it" (4.1.56). But it goes deeper than that, for Claudio's error points to the irrelevance here of the whole of the conventional moral argument about masks. This kind of unmasking is out of place because masks in the play are not moral masks. Even Don John the villain does not hide his malice beneath smiles but flaunts his surliness and ill will and is still believed. Equally out of place is the plain speaking and insulting language of the accusers ("a common stale," "this rotten orange"). Deep in error, the accusers have rejected wit, replacing it with what they think is true, but what we perceive to be an unfounded and hysterical leap into false morality.

The confrontation between Beatrice and Benedick that follows re-creates the genuine terms of the play's earlier movement between hidden feeling and displayed artifice, with a mask of wit as a device of interpretation between the two. Here, too, there is plain speaking. Beatrice weeps; they declare their belief in Hero and love for each other. Scorn, pity, and love are present but these real feelings do not make wit redundant. On the contrary, the genuine quality of the discovery and of the obligations ("Kill Claudio") it entails are strengthened by the survival of the stance of wit in the dialogue. The mask is lowered and feeling is revealed. But the ironic advantages of masking are not surrendered and make the confession subtle:

> *Benedick:* By my sword, Beatrice, thou lovest me.
> *Beatrice:* Do not swear and eat it.
>
> (4.1.274–75)

As the scene that sets out the serious possibilities of ending and contrasts two versions of the culminating act of unmasking, the church scene also restates and brings into contrast the moods and styles of expression that compete for dominance as the end approaches. On the simplest level the pathos of the shamed bride is balanced by the faith and experience of the Friar, who is supported by the as yet unrevealed turn of events. This is matter for the plot to turn into the happy ending. More difficult to resolve because it is not a matter of a turn of events is the tension between the false emotionalism of the young men's discovery and the serious wit of Beatrice and Benedick's confession. The very strange first scene of act 5 takes this tension to the point where it will be resolved in recognition of the truth, but not without the fiercely ironic exposure of false wit.

The unfortunate young men whose false feeling was a sign of their surrender of wit are here guilty of the opposite blunder. Their false wit is a sign of their lack of feeling, where feeling is in tune with the truth. The critical moment of Beatrice and Benedick's discovery displays the difficult balance between wit and feeling, mask and exposure that only they achieve. The confrontation between Claudio, Pedro, and Benedick (5.1) exposes an unanchored wit to the cool scrutiny of an unamused eye and serious mind. No one laughs as Claudio scores points off a victim who is not playing the game. Don Pedro's discovery, "He is in earnest" (5.1.194), is not taken up by Claudio, but just because it is not, it may be taken as a stronger signal to the audience of the emptiness of Claudio's wit. Indeed, Don Pedro's own words, intended as mockery of Benedick, betray the speaker:

> What a pretty thing man is when he goes in his doublet and hose and leaves off his wit!
>
> (5.1.199–200)

Benedick's earnestness is the opposite of the gallant's false wit. It is itself partly a pretense (Hero is not dead) but it makes clear at a moment of revelation a tension underlying the whole action: that confrontation between genuine feeling, though touched with artifice, and the elaborate play of wit. In the story of Beatrice and Benedick wit both fights and carries feeling. In the benevolent practice on their pride, the wit of the practicers even creates feeling. But the villainous practice of Don John upsets the balance by trapping the young men into both false feeling and false wit. The play, however, is not pressing for a choice to be made between wit and feeling. Such choices are the fruits of the gallant's error. Rather it seeks to establish at the end the balance between the two that is characteristic of Beatrice and Benedick.

The last two scenes of the play are built around two ceremonies, each of which embodies one side of this balance. The scene at the monument is a perfunctory ceremony of expiation, based on the minimal recognition of guilt by Claudio:

> . . . yet sinn'd I not,
> But in mistaking.
>
> (5.1.273–74)

The moan and groan of the "solemn hymn" are as far as this feeling can go: a confrontation with death to enable life to continue:

> *Don Pedro:* Come, let us hence, and put on other weeds, . . .
>
> (5.3.30)

The unmaskings of Hero and Beatrice are not perfunctory. They are climactic actions because they are the last in a series of similar acts, one a gross and almost tragic error, that form the backbone of the play. They are "reck'nings," as Claudio says (5.4.52), a comic reward in the discovery of the loved one and a comic punishment in the discovery of the practice against Beatrice and Benedick.

The first unmasking, Hero's, is simple, a return to truth and life and a relinquishing of pretense. It is the formal and moral opposite of Claudio's false discovery in the church scene. For Claudio the game of masking that caused him his first attack of precocious despair at the beginning of the play is over with this final choice. The partner he ends with is the same partner he despaired of, rejected, and now finally discovers.

The unmasking of Beatrice is less final and less simple. This unmasking also complements the earlier ones. In the church no physical mask was dropped, but Beatrice and Benedick, in the grip of genuine feeling for Hero, confessed their love for each other. Here at the end the dropping of the physical mask coincides with the revival or continuation of the battle that the mask symbolizes and that the opening masquerade set out so clearly.

The mask comes off to reveal no miracle but the two antagonists in their familiar pose, the discovery being that they were tricked. If the romantic unmasking reveals innocent love as a familiar wonder, a gift undeserved but granted to Claudio for his beauty and youth, its parody reveals the consistent traits of character that make the happy ending work on a more realistic level. Benedick the married man is not transformed, and neither is Beatrice. Marriage has become Benedick's "humor"—a witty way of protecting feeling against wit. So this unmasking does not simplify the character it dispatches to the final dance. Rather it preserves the tensions of artifice against feeling, of word against act, as a counter to the pat conclusion of the other story. Benedick's conclusion—"for man is a giddy thing" (5.4.108)—is robustly comic because it goes beyond the bourgeois convention of symmetry at the happy end and dwells instead on the irrational gaiety and disorder that the dances and ceremonies of ending are supposed to tame.

Why should *As You Like It* end? This may be an odd question from a playgoer's point of view but a possibly enlightening one if it makes us think about peculiarities of the play's structure. The first thing one might notice about this structure is that once the scene has moved to the forest neither characters nor events are really moving in any defined direction whatsoever. The forest is not a place where people search for each other, so losing and finding is not a principle of articulation in the plot, as it is in *A Midsummer Night's Dream*. It is rather a place where groups of people are set down in proximity, meeting casually. "Look you, who comes here" (2.4.19–20) is the characteristic linking phrase between encounters. There is no particular reason why these encounters should stop. Discovery here is not founded on the tension of a necessary meeting delayed to the very end. Rosalind confronts Orlando early on in her forest career; she even meets her father and the smooth tenor of the plot remains undisturbed.

The casual rhythm of the encounters juxtaposed in a linear sequence is peculiar as a comic rhythm. It does not have the mounting frenzy of a race against time, nor is there a progression toward the kind of climax produced by an intrigue. The obstacles in the way of the lovers' happiness are not created by an evil design that has to be overcome. All these negatives mean that although the untying of the knot—Rosalind's unmasking—is conventional enough, the deadlock that makes the unmasking necessary is reached in a less conventional way.

The impasse that precedes unmasking is set out graphically in a stage picture comically expressive in its own right but also characteristic of the play's linear method. In 5.2 Phebe, Orlando, and Silvius whine their litany of unrequited love in a formal sequence. Their differences of character, sex, and status are submerged in a democracy of frustrated love that gives each the same bleating phrase:

> *Silvius:*   And so am I for Phebe.
> *Phebe:*   And I for Ganymed.
> *Orlando:*   And I for Rosalind.
>
> (5.2.90–92)

The action implied here is a gesture in the direction of the unobtainable beloved—Silvius to Phebe, Phebe to Ganymed, and Orlando to Ganymed, the Rosalind of his pretense. Rosalind, as befits her part in the complication of the action, is both inside this formal sequence and detached from it. She repeats the phrase, she is subject to the feelings described by Silvius, but her repetition is on the surface a denial: "And I for no woman" (5.2.88). She breaks the sequence by capping it, by turning it for us from a lineup of equals to an arrangement with a secret meaning that only she can supply. This is even more clear in the last round of repetitions: "If this be so, why blame you me to love you?" (5.2.103). The questions have to be asked of someone, and again the sequence stops at Rosalind, who breaks the hypnotic rhythm by challenging Orlando:

> Why do you speak too, "Why blame you me to love you?"
> (5.2.106–7)

She goes on to replace the pattern of frustrations with her own pattern of solutions:

> . . . As you love Rosalind, meet. As you love Phebe, meet. And as I love no woman, I'll meet. So fare you well, I have left you commands.
>
> (5.2.118–21)

The scene's structure is typical of that of the whole play in that it proceeds by juxtaposing characters who are in similar situations, subjecting them to the single complicating device of Rosalind's disguise. More in control and less compromised by the action than most other comic protagonists in Shakespeare, Rosalind alone dictates the appropriate moment of ending:

> To-morrow meet me all together.
> (5.2.112)

This is also the simplest structural principle of the play, which brings to the center of the stage in sequence contrasting groups of characters, lovers of different rank and style, exiles of different philosophical persuasions, and the natural inhabitants of the pastoral scene, thus making juxtaposition the moving force instead of intrigue. While an intrigue usually presses toward some target, a climax, or resolution, a sequence of contrasted situations is more static, possibly ironic, and less pregnant with resolution. This is the impression given by *As You Like It* if one comes to it after the chases of *The Comedy of Errors* or *A Midsummer Night's Dream,* or the struggle with an evil will in the tragicomedies. It is reinforced by the nature of the pastoral setting, which provides a frame for discussion rather than a maze of error.

The verbal style of the play also shows analogies to the linearity of the scene sequences. The catalogue speeches and the speeches that allocate their separate fate to the contrasted groups of lovers show how the wit of the play delights in the shape of the series. At the drop of a hat characters will produce a list of contrasts such as Rosalind's list:

> . . . who Time ambles withal, who Time trots withal, who Time gallops withal, and who he stands still withal.
> (3.2.309–11)

There is also Jaques's list of the parts played in a lifespan and Touchstone's catalogue of the history of a courtly quarrel. The wit of most of these catalogue speeches has an anticlimactic quality. The speeches do not push for conclusions, and even when they do, as Jaques tries to with his—

> . . . Last scene of all,
> That ends this strange eventful history, . . .
> (2.7.163–64)

—his conclusion "sans every thing" is contested by the very next action: Orlando enters with Adam, an image of old age protected and served by youth.

Touchstone is the master of the ironic refusal of climax, notably in his elaboration on the stages of a quarrel that never came to proof, but also in his display of how to avoid a straight answer to Corin's simple question:

And how like you this shepherd's life, Master Touchstone?
Touchstone: Truly, shepherd, in respect of itself, it is a good life;
but in respect that it is a shepherd's life, it is naught. In
respect that it is solitary, I like it very well; but in
respect that it is private, it is a very vild life.
(3.2.11–17)

Touchstone's march of contraries, a fool's dialectic, is the opposite of
Corin's plain speaking. It hovers around a choice without making it,
using the language of discrimination to camouflage a set piece of witty
aggression on a countryman. The fool presses to the extreme the kind
of game that Rosalind plays with Orlando. This is also a dizzying
parade of change and opposites in speech and action:

. . . effeminate, changeable, longing and liking, proud, fantastical,
apish, shallow, inconstant, full of tears, full of smiles; for every
passion something, and for no passion truly any thing . . . .
(3.2.410–14)

Corin's directness is like the directness of true love, an immediate
expression of true and natural feelings. Rosalind's double personality
hides the honest frankness of a Corin under the witty mask of a Touchstone, subjecting the natural revelation to the delaying logic of the
game.
    This game is the cure of Orlando, and it gives their meetings in the
forest a shape and apparent purpose. The exhaustion of the game coin-
ciding with the deadlock of the lovers is the signal for the unmasking:

Orlando: I can live no longer by thinking.
Rosalind: I will weary you then no longer with idle talking.
(5.2.50–52)

The game is an arbitrary device of Rosalind, and its tension derives
from the artificial delaying of the revelation of feeling and identity,
which craves immediate expression. At its simplest, romantic love is
kindled in a flash and seeks immediate consummation. Lovers wish the
end to be as close to the beginning as circumstances allow. This is the
lucky case of Celia and Oliver, who:

. . . no sooner met but they look'd; no sooner look'd but they lov'd;
no sooner lov'd but they sigh'd; no sooner sigh'd but they ask'd one
another the reason; no sooner knew the reason but they sought the
remedy: . . .
(5.2.33–37)

There, mocked by Rosalind's wit, is the simple progression of true love towards its goal, like climbing stairs. None of the traditional obstacles manages to hinder the forward march. Rosalind's game, on the other hand, dramatizes some of the difficulties of reaching this goal by using wit willfully to put off an end that is always tantalizingly close and yet somehow turns into its opposite:

Orlando: Then love me, Rosalind.
Rosalind: Yes, faith, will I, Fridays and Saturdays and all.
Orlando: And wilt thou have me?
Rosalind: Ay, and twenty such.
Orlando: What sayest thou?
Rosalind: Are you not good?
Orlando: I hope so.
Rosalind: Why then can one desire too much of a good thing?
                                                              (4.1.115–24)

Touchstone can perform this way without betraying strain, but Rosalind's turns of wit at the expense of feeling are an affectation whose victories have to be paid for by her collapse into feminine softness and tears between the bouts: "I'll go find a shadow, and sigh till he come." (4.1.216–17). In this way the sequence of meetings reveals an inner tension that must force an end—unmasking. The "saucy Lackey" who approached her victim with a baited question concealing a witty catalogue of time's subjects is soon herself a victim of time, jealous of every minute her lover spends out of her sight:

How say you now? Is it not past two a'clock? And here much Orlando!

                                                              (4.3.1–2)

Time, though not at all a factor in the action (morning, noon, and evening are indistinguishable in the forest), begins to be measured out in thousandths of a minute as the spaces between Orlando's appearances get more burdensome for Rosalind and the game harder to play.

Rosalind's decision to throw off her mask is then of a different quality from her decision to don it. The one is the opening move in the game; she controls it. The other is more a forced move, made necessary both by the demands of her own nature rebelling against the mask and the refusal of her partner to carry on.

The denouement of *As You Like It* is simple, as befits the lack of complication in the action that ties the knot. One change turns the impasse of 5.2 into the country copulatives of the end. This change is heavily prepared for, twice rehearsed verbally in Rosalind's summaries of each character's dilemma and her promised solution (5.2.; 5.4).

When the change comes it does so as a rational climax, the final turn in a repeated series that lacks meaning without it:

> *Hymen:* Peace, ho! I bar confusion,
> 'Tis I must make conclusion
> Of these most strange events.
>
> (5.4.125–27)

The confusions of masking leave no mark on the formality of this revelation. Reason does diminish wonder, as Hymen says. Each relationship is defined in sequence, daughter to father, wife to husband, lover to lover. Each couple is labeled in accordance with its position on the map of love. So Hymen says to Touchstone and Audrey:

> You and you are sure together,
> As the winter to foul weather.
>
> (5.4.135–36)

It is an expected end and at its center stand Hymen and Rosalind, figures of control and release whose perspective is stable.

The turbulence and confusion so lacking in this revelation are introduced as an afterthought by Jaques De Boys with his surprising news of Duke Frederick's violent plan and his sudden conversion.

The play, then, ends on the contrast between two kinds of change. In the foreground is the rational expected change of Rosalind's unmasking that helps make earthly things even. In the background is the miraculous irrational conversion of an evil man, which changes everything. It will move the nobles out of the forest and reconstitute the situation as it was before the play began. The Duke chooses to emphasize the first, smaller change:

> First, in this forest let us do those ends
> That here were well begun and well begot; . . .
>
> (5.4.170–71)

Jaques, by his lone exit, draws attention to the more mysterious change, which is not the result of the comic device but of a miracle. Two patterns here contribute to ending in contrasting ways. One is man-made, the game of Rosalind's masking that was in her power to stop. This is the content of most of the action. The other is providential and cataclysmic. It puts the repentant Duke in the forest and snatches Duke Senior out of it. The connection between miracle and device, here arbitrary, is the essence of change in the romances.

Twelfth Night occupies a central position in the pattern of Shake-

speare's comedy. It looks both backward and forward; backward to
The Comedy of Errors and the Italianate and Roman traditions of errors and disguising,[20] but also forward to the miraculous recognitions of
the romances. It includes the motif of evil and death, stated more
subtly than in *Much Ado* because it is independent of any evil will, but
inherent in the situation of frustrated love and the device of the mask.
The play exploits to the full, in the manner of *The Comedy of Errors,*
the riotous possibilities of mistaken identity, but imagines with far
more subtlety the price paid both by those who are mistaken and by
Viola, who is the prisoner of her assumed sex.

The sense of being trapped, of a knot that cannot be untied, is already a factor of the opening situations. Orsino is shown caught in a
hopeless passion and Olivia is exposed in her irrational and possibly
specious refusal of the world, which is in fact a refusal of one man's
love. There is no evil in this immobility, but it has a sterile quality that
links it to the finality of death. It is death in the sense that love
unfulfilled seals youth and beauty prematurely with the mark of the
grave, the mark of fruitlessness, as Viola points out to Olivia in her first
interview:

> Lady, you are the cruell'st she alive
> If you will lead these graces to the grave,
> And leave the world no copy.
>
> (1.5.241–43)

The constancy of the initial deadlock is the structural backbone of
the play because it generates the repetitive movement of Viola between
the two households, a movement whose very mechanism displays the
helplessness of all three entangled characters:

> All the occurrence of my fortune since
> Hath been between this lady and this lord.
>
> (5.1.257–58)

If the initial impasse is the inexplicable and irrational refusal of the
beloved, countered by the obstinate persistence of the lover, this is
further complicated by the entry into the scene of the disguised Viola.
Her intervention fills with life the deathlike situation of the opening.
She unfreezes the passion locked up by Olivia's unnatural refusal. She
alters our sense of Orsino by falling in love with him. On the other
hand, her intervention makes the entanglement more hopeless. It introduces the wickedness of disguise that becomes a trap and reduces
the awareness of Viola to an awareness of the desperateness of her
situation, the hopelessness of her master's love, and the absurdity of

Olivia's passion. The great advance from the mistakings of *The Comedy of Errors* and *A Midsummer Night's Dream* is that the causes of the impasse are understood by the character, who concentrates in herself the true perception of the play. But her knowledge is limited by her entrapment in the situation, like the other victims. She has no devices, though she is the only conscious disguiser. In fact, her passivity is extreme:

> O time, thou must untangle this, not I,
> It is too hard a knot for me t'untie.
>
> (2.2.40–41)

Twelfth Night, more than all the other romantic comedies, poses the question of the discrepancy between the tying and the untying actions, the hard knot and the way in which it is loosened. Such a discrepancy does not appear in *As You Like It* because of Rosalind's control of the game and because of the absence of pain and real difficulty in the masking. It is also absent in a play like *The Comedy of Errors,* because the lucid design peeps reassuringly through every chaotic movement. There the progression toward union is totally apparent to us, though the characters cannot be aware of it.

Twelfth Night has neither the transparent design of the early play nor the sense of purpose given to *As You Like It* by Rosalind's energy. This is because the involvement at its center is not one that intelligence can untangle. As Viola says to Olivia:

> In your denial I would find no sense,
> I would not understand it.
>
> (1.5.266–67)

It is an involvement like that of the crazed lovers in the forest of *A Midsummer Night's Dream*—irrational, violent, exposing infatuation shamelessly—but there is no mechanism of love potions to explain its origins and to suggest a way out.

The way out is, of course, Sebastian, the person created for solution. He is the device the playwright and providence are keeping in reserve. But Sebastian's entry into the maze of misunderstandings in act 4 complicates matters before it unties the knot. He is as much a victim of this situation as the others, even though his reactions to both amorous and physical assault are healthy. A study of the untying action of the play would not, then, concentrate solely on Sebastian's progress; rather it would point to the way the motif of recognition, through a series of disappointments and failures, creates a characteristic rhythm of ending, a sequence of violent checks that modulate into a liberating confrontation.

The deadlock at the heart of the play is given graphic if caricatured expression in a scene that is the cue for the first in the series of failed recognitions marking the unwinding rhythm of the action. The device of the duel between Viola and Sir Andrew is an offshoot of the comic energy that gulls Malvolio. But the stage picture of the natural fool and the masquerading girl facing each other with drawn swords is important for its own sake. It summarizes the impasse in all its absurdity. The pent-up violence of the rejected lovers is present in the drawn swords and the threat of wounding. The unreality under which Olivia and Orsino labor finds its analogy in the absurd confrontation of coward and girl that brings Viola as close as she ever comes to revealing herself before the end:

> A little thing would make me tell them how much I lack of a man.
> (3.4.302–3)

This moment, then, a transposition of the knot of the play into a minor mode, a moment of immobility (each participant is imprisoned in his own fear) and threatened riot (the proposed duel), is interrupted by the first of the failed recognitions that make up the modulating action. They do this by piecing together the truth while contributing to the sense of increasing craziness.

The opening move is Antonio's. In his selfless act of friendship for "Sebastian" he defines himself:

> One, sir, that for his love dares yet do more
> Than you have heard him brag to you he will.
> (3.4.316–17)

He is recognized by the officer—"I know your favor well" (3.4.329)—but is denied by Viola: "Nor know I you by voice or any feature" (3.4.353).

The genuine pathos and anger of his reaction are based on something nearer the truth than either Olivia's or Orsino's experience. They are hurt by the refusal of the object of their passion to conform to their idea of it. He is wounded by a doubleness in the object itself. It drives him toward madness. But his passion, founded on something unreal, gives birth to hope in Viola. In her perception of them, his unbelievable words can herald the truth of what was only till then a wish: "Prove true, imagination, O, prove true" (3.4.375). False recognition in Antonio, then, yields a partial recognition of the truth in Viola, and craziness, pathos and anger on the one hand are balanced by hope on the other.

The next recognition is a very close parallel in terms of stage gesture and similar in that it also yields a mixture of madness and truth. In 4.1 Olivia bursts in on the threatened duel between Sebastian and Sir Toby, just as Antonio did in the previous case. This time the violence is far more real. Sebastian has already beaten Sir Andrew, and there is no pretense behind his drawn sword. It is an image of riot rather than deadlock, and Olivia's interruption breaks the pattern of impasse that has ruled the love relationships till now. She is overwhelmingly successful where she has always failed. Unlike Antonio's, her assumption of recognition is not denied. It seems unreal to Sebastian, like madness or a dream, but in submitting to the lady's desire he chooses this unreality because of what it promises.

These two parallel confrontations, one pathetic, the other successful, have juxtaposed emergent truth, dreams of pleasure, and plot-induced mistakes of identity. The wrong recognitions produce hints of, and indeed, lead the way to resolution. The irrational behavior of a strange lady with Sebastian produces tangible things that can be observed and stand the test of the light of day:

> This is the air, that is the glorious sun,
> This pearl she gave me, I do feel't and see't, . . .

$$(4.3.1-2)$$

Such recognitions are both real and unreal. They cannot be understood by those who try. They breed confusion, madness, disappointment, and hope but through them we recognize the unfolding pattern that is to lead to the final recognition and resolution.

The opening of act 5 restates the trap of failed recognitions, together with the impasse of love with which the play opened. Untying the knot is not a simple progression towards discovery. There is no waking up or chase to mark the steps forward. Instead, the coming together of all the central characters except Sebastian makes the difficulty and seriousness of the tangle apparent again, just as its resolution is about to appear. It is the obstinate immobility of the play's opening that marks the meeting of Orsino and Olivia:

> *Duke:*　Still so cruel?
> *Olivia:*　Still so constant, lord.

$$(5.1.110-11)$$

Everything seems to militate against the possibility of change. Recognition (Olivia and Viola, Antonio and Viola) is cruelly false. Frustration threatens to become violent as the Duke contemplates revenge. The mood veers between the ironic distance created by rhyming couplets and the pathos of the revelations and denials. Again and again the language returns to the puzzle of identity: "Hast thou forgot thyself?" (5.1.141), "Be that thou know'st thou art" (5.1.149). Everyone is bound up in this puzzle, even the Priest, despite the authoritative way he describes the wedding ceremony. But behind the violence and the impasse we sense the approach of resolution. The staggered and staggering entrances of Sir Andrew and Sir Toby are violent evidence of Sebastian's proximity. Their wounds are a reality that demand an agent and when Sebastian enters the scene he does so both as a miracle and as the final piece in a puzzle.

The humanity of Shakespeare's treatment of recognition in *Twelfth Night* lies in his balancing of the madness and violence of a farcelike situation of mistakings, division, and impasse with a sense of the seriousness, mystery, and healing powers of true recognition.

This mystery and healing quality cannot, as in *The Comedy of Errors,* spring mainly from the providential appearance of a figure who ties beginning to end and symbolizes the restoration of unity to a divided family. The family theme is here subordinate to the love tangle. The twin who is incomplete without his brother can find in the sight of his double the full identity denied him by accident. *The Comedy of Errors* makes us expect and desire reunion rather than change. In *Twelfth Night,* however, Orsino's refusal to accept reality and Olivia's infatuation with a mask need to undergo a change if the knot is to be untied. This change is not explicit; no magic transforms them. The Duke's violence and Olivia's pathos and rejection state the recalcitrance of misunderstanding on the very threshold of resolution. But it is an overliteral reading of the play that would rob the discoveries brought by Sebastian of their significance for all the major participants. Sebastian is not only the glass in which Viola is reflected but also the mirror that restores identity to Olivia and Antonio. His address to Olivia is simple:

> Pardon me, sweet one, even for the vows
> We made each other but so late ago.
>
> (5.1.214–15)

but its resonance is great. In a play so full of address frustrated by error[21] and of truth condemned to silence by disguise, his naming of Olivia and Antonio in terms of true relationships and a real past is to release them from the spell of ignorance. It is wonder rather than surprise that accompanies Sebastian's entry. There is no unmasking. No one changes visibly and the stage action is kept to a minimum. Twice we are told that the twins will *not* embrace, once before the discovery—

> *Sebastian:* Were you a woman, as the rest goes even,
> I should my tears let fall upon your cheek,
>
> (5.1.239–40)

and once after it:

> *Viola:* Do not embrace me till each circumstance
> Of place, time, fortune, do cohere and jump
> That I am Viola.
>
> (5.1.251–53)

Viola in the most important refusal of change remains in her boy's disguise, Cesario, till the end. Recognition is thus strangely muted.[22] It is the silence after the storm, and whether the approach to knowledge is marked step-by-step as in the discovery dialogue of Sebastian and Viola, or the revolution worked by knowledge is implied by silence (as in Olivia's case), we assent to it as a mystery rather than a trick. Sebastian's "You are betroth'd both to a maid and man" (5.1.263) sounds at first as if it could be a line from *Epicoene*. But it refers to the pattern behind the chaos, "Nature to her bias drew in that" (5.1.260), more than it does to the error, "So comes it, lady, you have been mistook" (5.1.259).

The end of *Twelfth Night* manages to hold together harmony and disharmony, resolution and what militates against it, change and recalcitrance. Malvolio's entrance and exit bluntly state what is left unresolved, curiously related to Viola's feminine attire. The processional exit, leaving Viola's sexual ambiguity unchanged, is a succinct picture of both the cause of the confusion as well as its solution. The endings of the romantic comedies all balance change and constancy. Their resolutions hold up before our eyes both what is consistent and what is transformed. The victorious metamorphosis of Rosalind does not alter either Jaques's refusal of festivity or the fragility of Touchstone's marriage. This balance of change and constancy is most subtly present at the end of *Twelfth Night,* for the absence of visual transformation or any other gesture of change makes the pairing off into couples share the stage with the persistence of sexual ambiguity in the central character.

Psychological and moral consistency often militate against a tidy happy ending, and many of the endings I have discussed are flexible

enough to include whatever is recalcitrant to change without surren-
dering to irony. In *Twelfth Night* the light emerges from the dark in a
way that neither violates the reality of the characters' mistakes nor
denies the essentially benevolent movement through error and illusion
to a rearrangement of partners and a corresponding fixing of identity in
terms of true relationships.[23] Artfulness, on display in the increased
pace and absurd contradictions of the final two acts, partly distances
the characters and their plight from us. But artfulness of another kind is
evident at the confrontation of the twins. Here it is nature's art, the
wondrous trick of doubleness and the miracle of the twin escape from
death, that encourages us to take the ending seriously. This sense of
the miraculous even makes it possible for us to find a poetic resonance
in the old formulas of recognition by birthmark:

> *Viola:*   My father had a mole upon his brow.
> *Sebastian:* And so had mine.
>
>   (5.1.242–43)

They are integrated into a purposeful rhythm of life and death, a
father's death and his children's seeming death and survival.

Shakespeare's awareness and exploitation of the formulas and conventions of happy ending are never more obvious than in the romances. The conscious art of the playwright forging a comic resolution
by patiently following the eventual consequences of apparent disaster
is inherent in the very structure of those plays that span lengths of time
(*The Winter's Tale* and *Pericles*). It is present in the character of the
plotter-artist Prospero who is given by Providence a scene, characters,
and a fixed time span in which he is free to bring about his drastic or
beneficent catastrophe. It is present on a lower level in the bravura
display of artifice and dramatic juggling in the denouement scene of
Cymbeline. Two of these plays end with scenes that draw attention
specifically to their own theatricality, to the trick element in dramatic
spectacle. Prospero and Paulina both unveil tableaux of the supposed
dead who come to life, to the amazement of their audience.

In *The Tempest* we share Prospero's knowledge because we have
observed him in the conniving of the various wonders and miracles.
But in *The Winter's Tale* we share the ignorance of Paulina's stage
audience in the statue scene. It is there that the seemingly naive desire
of the audience to have things come out well in spite of the evidence is
gratified by a coup de théâtre that sums up many of the motifs and
features of the Shakespearean happy ending.

Comic actions cannot deal with the finality of death unless it is a
pretense, as in the mock tactical deaths of Hero in *Much Ado* and

Claudio in *Measure for Measure*. Yet the very presence of the tactical death and resurrection as a device in comic plots hints at the deep and irrational wish underlying much comedy that the most recalcitrant feature of our natural life, our mortality, be cancelled. In other words, that we live happily ever after. Death is an illusion, this device seems to say, an instructive illusion like all suffering in romantic comedy. It is there to make us savor more fully what is real, namely union in love and friendship and the restoration of relationships broken by time, error, or malice. In *Much Ado,* much of the tension of the closing action rises out of the failure of the device to awaken guilt in the erring accusers. Hero's seeming death awakens Benedick, who knows it is a device, rather than Claudio, whose wit is made to look wildly out of place in the shadow of death. There our awareness of the device arms us with detachment. Our interest is mostly in a critical observation of the young men, for the end, thanks to Dogberry, is not in doubt. In *The Winter's Tale,* on the other hand, the stroke of death appears to be final and it enters the play in a pivotal scene to seemingly deny the hope of any other ending than a tragic one.

The ending of the action initiated by Leontes' jealousy and the beginning of the one initiated by Perdita's survival are marked by three catastrophic blows of death. The prophecy of the oracle " 'and the King shall live without an heir, if that which is lost be not found' " (3.2.134–36) is followed by news of the Prince's death and shortly after that, by Paulina's report of Hermione's death. These two announcements envelope and mock the sudden awakening of Leontes to the monstrosity of his action. Leontes, asking pardon of the god, imagines wildly a happy ending in the midst of disaster:

> I'll reconcile me to Polixenes,
> New woo my queen, recall the good Camillo,
> Whom I proclaim a man of truth, of mercy;
>
> (3.2.155–57)

This desperate desire to avoid the consequences of evil actions is subverted by the reality of death that Paulina describes as the impossibility of any miraculous return to life:

> . . . If you can bring
> Tincture or lustre in her lip, her eye,
> Heat outwardly or breath within, I'll serve you
> As I would do the gods.
>
> (3.2.204–7)

Indeed, the scene ends with the expectation of a penance that is to last as long as life. However, the tied knot of Leontes' hopeless recognition of his guilt is set alongside the beginning of the untying action. The scene of the abandoning of Perdita (3.3) is both end and beginning and, as such, it alters the perspective of the play from a tragic one, which isolates the irrevocable consequences of an act of wrong to a comic one, which enables us to see beyond those consequences by taking the story further. Life and death, beginning and ending, comedy and tragedy are held in the balance in this scene, which deals out a stern and impersonal account of moral responsibility to Antigonus and the hapless sailors, while Perdita is saved and chosen for life. The end of the men is both absurd and a mystery. Antigonus's demise is foretold by the apparition of Hermione in his dream. But the means of his death is as eccentric as it is savage. The sailors are drowned under dim and disapproving skies. Both catastrophes, as told by the neutral Clown, have an element of mockery in them. The sea mocks the sailor and the bear mocks its victim. This is cruel mockery, and death is dwelt upon in great though humorous detail:

> . . . The men are not yet cold under water, nor the bear half din'd on
> the gentleman. He's at it now.
>
> (3.3.105–6)

But the finality of death is balanced by the discovery of what has survived nature's impartial savagery. Death picks out its victims but their catastrophe falls into a pattern defined by Time as something as yet incomplete. The nature of this pattern is not yet clear. Time is an equivocal force. In *Twelfth Night* Viola's cry is a naive appeal for a happy end to an impossible situation:

> O time, thou must untangle this, not I,
> It is too hard a knot for me t'untie.
>
> (*Twelfth Night,* 2.2.40–41)

In *The Winter's Tale,* Time (the Chorus) promises no specific end. He not only unfolds error, but he also makes it. His perspective is inclusive of all and therefore neutral. He plants and overwhelms, being constant only to himself. He is neither on the side of youth nor its enemy. As a witness he promises nothing but change. Thus he cannot be the agent of ending; some other force will be called on to turn death into life.

The second half of the play is as full of devices as the first half is free of them. The characteristic irony of the first part is in the mockery of circumstances, as the bear and the sea mock their victims. Significant reaction to Leontes' drastic steps is initiated by the gods, while catastrophe arises out of nature. In the second part the progress towards ending is dependent on the active intervention of plotters, benevolent practicers like Camillo and not so benevolent ones like Autolycus. Camillo's plan to win Leontes' protection for Florizel and Perdita envisages an end in keeping with the pain of the past:

> . . . . Methinks I see
> Leontes opening his free arms, and weeping
> His welcomes forth; asks thee there, son, forgiveness,
> As 't'were i'th'father's person; kisses the hands
> Of your fresh princess; o'er and o'er divides him
> 'Twixt his unkindness and his kindness:
>
> (4.4.547–52)

But all this is based on deceit. Camillo's practice, in which Autolycus plays a minor part (his exchange of clothes with Florizel) and a major one (bringing the agents of recognition on board ship), is the force that in the second half of the play replaces the impersonal moving powers of the action. Instead of the wind and the sea to which Florizel would commit himself in desperation, he surrenders himself wisely to the theatrical art of Camillo. He is given a scene to play in which Perdita is also to "bear a part." That the deceit is the bearer of truth is a secret that only we know.

The ending of *The Winter's Tale* shows a powerful and moving conflict between the expressive but also naive tools of the poet of the theater and the recalcitrance of the human conduct he has chosen for his subject. This recalcitrance is centered not in character, for Leontes has changed, but in the consequences of his error. Death is no device, and 5.1 restates the impasse created by Hermione's death in blunt terms.

> *Paulina:* If, one by one, you wedded all the world,
> Or, from the all that are, took something good
> To make a perfect woman, she you kill'd
> Would be unparallel'd.
>
> (5.1.13–16)

Evans[24] is wrong, when he finds in this scene a suggestion that the playwright is regretting his refusal of knowledge to the audience and is smuggling us the information of Hermione's survival, hoping it will not be too obvious. The power of the end absolutely depends on our certainty about Hermione's death and the conflict between this certainty and the irrational wish that it were not so. As it is, the first in the series of encounters that marks the approach to the statue scene (5.1) abounds in echoes that link it to the earlier confrontations in the play. Perdita's praise in the mouth of the Gentleman evokes the memory of Hermione and his earlier praise of her now-forgotten beauty. Florizel is so like Polixenes that Leontes is tempted to cancel the intervening gap of time and call the young man brother. The sight of the young pair reminds Leontes of his own "dead" children, who "Might thus have stood, begetting wonder" (5.1.133). Finally Leontes, with unconscious irony, links the journey of Perdita from Bohemia to Sicilia with her first journey, which should have been to her death:

> . . . . And hath he too
> Expos'd this paragon to th' fearful usage,
> (At least ungentle) of the dreadful Neptune,
>
> (5.1.152–54)

These correspondences and echoes express both loss and its opposite. Florizel's arrival recalls the dead prince but Perdita's beauty, while evoking the lost grace of Hermione, also reminds us of what has secretly been saved:

> *Leontes:* . . . I thought of her,
> Even in these looks I made.
>
> (5.1.227–28)

There is a symmetry here akin to the doublings at the end of many comedies, but the presence of death makes it a symmetry between the living and the dead, between a present that recalls the past teasingly and makes it live again, if only in wish or in desire, as in Leontes' look at Perdita.

The full resuscitation of the past is the work of the great scene of miraculous transformation. But we cannot fully understand the powerful theatricality of that ending without a consideration of the clearly contrasted group of narrated recognitions (5.2) that precedes it. As is well known, the editor of the New Cambridge Shakespeare thought the transposition of the recognition was the "greatest fault of all"[25] in a play that he found generally disappointing. Later critics, notably Coghill, have defended the narration on the grounds of theatrical expediency. Coghill is right when he notices that the messenger speeches generate "that mounting thrill of expectation needed to prepare us for the final scene."[26] But close attention to these descriptions of recognition reveals what kind of preparation and contrast this is.

The contrast is primarily between language and action, between the thing itself and its interpretation. In the narration we are continually being reminded of the intensity of an experience that defeats capture in words. The Gentlemen are the audience who observe large actions, like the embracing and the holding up of hands, or much smaller actions without movement like the long look of recognition between Leontes and Camillo. These are culminating and meaningful actions, but their very intensity blurs distinction. The beholder cannot say "if th' importance were joy or sorrow" (5.2.18), nor can the faces of the kings be distinguished from each other in their ecstasy. The experience eludes description because of its intensity, but also because of its fusing of opposites. Joy and loss, kissing and weeping, one eye declined, the other elevated; this is an excess of expressive action and feeling that the elaborate prose of the spectators can imitate only with a conscious effort. Despite all the words we are left with a sense of something unexpressed. The intervening verbal screen whets our appetite for the sight itself. The audience of kings and princes is too restricted when we are in the theater to watch just such actions and interpret them for ourselves.

After the exaggerated imagined actions of the crowded scene of recognitions has filtered through the words of the gentlemen, the scene of transformation is presented as an isolated act performed before one audience, integrating the stage spectators with those in the theater in a common curiosity and wonder. Whatever discovery takes place there, it is ours as well as that of the characters. No more does superfluous language interpose itself between the action and its meaning. Our only advantage over Leontes is knowledge that the statue is not stone but an actor, the same actor or actress who has played the part of the living Hermione. The unveiling of the statue is both a confrontation with death and a reminder of the theatrical artifice that robs death of its finality. The presence of death is never so central at the end of Shakespeare's comedies as it is here. Elsewhere, death is a patent illusion or a didactic trick played by Providence. Here it is the central fact set out in a statue that silently proclaims what might have been, that conquers time by its stony persistence and yet, oddly, shows the wrinkles of the passing of sixteen years.

The confrontation with the statue restates the tragic knot of the first part and simultaneously arouses a strong wish that the knot be miraculously untied. The movement of the dialogue, as the statue is hungrily observed by us and the characters, is not toward recognition but toward the discovery of life. This trick-miracle goes beyond all the revelations of Shakespeare's last scenes because its dependence on a manipulating mind is minimal. As William Matchett says, "it is a miracle in the full effect of which we participate."[27]

It is fitting that this play, with its arbitrary theatricality, its patent manipulation of time, and its persistent references to its own incredibility should end with the most artificial of conclusions that is yet one of the most stable and satisfactory in Shakespeare's work. Comedies of all kinds need minor miracles to undo their knots of folly and error. The miracle worker is usually the comic playwright himself, consciously engineering solutions. We hear the word *miracle* at the end of Jonson's satire as well as in the surprising denouements of Molière. But Jonson's and Molière's miracles cannot be taken seriously. We do not find any real correspondences between their cunning art and patterns that are more than human. In Shakespeare's comedies, the magic, the coincidences, and the devices that lead to resolution keep us aware of the part played by art in contriving the happy end. But this is an art that despite its transparency and its transience as performance redeems itself not only by gratifying our desire for pleasure but by giving us grounds for belief.

Notes

CHAPTER 1

1. A study of the strategies of ending in poetry is Barbara Herrnstein Smith's *Poetic Closure* (Chicago, 1968).
2. See ibid. on failures of closure, 210–34.
3. Northrop Frye in his *Anatomy of Criticism* (Princeton, N.J., 1971), 164, says that resolution in comedies emerges essentially from the wish of the audience.
4. See Marvin T. Herrick, *Comic Theory in the Sixteenth Century* (Urbana, Ill., 1964), 122–29, for a useful summary of discussions of comic ending in the postclassical commentators. A study that deals briefly with denouement on the Elizabethan and Jacobean stage in the light of the formal theory of Guarini, Castelvetro, and Minturno is Madeleine Doran's *Endeavors of Art* (Madison, Wisc., 1964), 322–31.
5. Aristotle, *Poetics*, in S. H. Butcher, trans., *Aristotle's Theory of Poetry and Fine Art* (London, 1911), 47–49.
6. Comedies that do not have happy endings, like Molière's *George Dandin*, may stress the necessity of their protagonist's defeat. The structure of repetition here is the structure of a trap, of expectation continually reversed.
7. Baudelaire in *De L'Essence du Rire* memorably describes the effect on him of a pantomime that aptly demonstrates this kind of rhythm. In the course of his distinction between the significantly and the absolutely comic (the former biased towards realism, the latter towards the grotesque) he relates how the pantomime clown, a knavish thief, is finally beheaded. But death cannot put an end to his thievery. The headless trunk carries on its manic labor and scoops up the severed head as yet another piece of booty. *Ecrits sur l'Art*, Vol. 1 (Paris, 1971), 319.
8. Horace, *Epistles*, 2.1.139–55, Loeb Classics (London, 1942).
9. John Gay, *The Beggar's Opera*, ed. John Hampden (London, 1964). In 3.16 the Player objects to the execution of Macheath on the grounds that "an opera must end happily." The Beggar agrees with him and gets the rabble to "run and cry a reprieve."
10. Plato, *Republic*, 10.606, in *The Dialogues of Plato*, trans. B. Jowett (Oxford, 1892), Vol. 3.
11. Sir Philip Sidney, *Works*, ed. W. Gray (London, 1893), 90.
12. Elder Olson, *The Theory of Comedy* (Bloomington, Ind., 1968), 36–37.
13. Aristotle, *Poetics*, 5:21.
14. John Dryden, *Essays*, ed. W. P. Ker (Oxford, 1926), 1:45.
15. Frye, in *Anatomy of Criticism*, 169–71, sees the movement of comedy both as a movement from a rigid society controlled by age to a freer society controlled by youth, and as a return to a kind of golden age presumed to have existed before the action of the play began.
16. Aristotle, *Poetics*, 18:65. Aristotle uses the terms *complication* and *unraveling* about tragedy.

17. Herrick *Comic Theory*, 106–7, traces the threefold division of comic plots to Donatus's commentary on Terence.

18. Donatus, *Aeli Donati quod fertur commentum Terenti, recensuit Paulus Wessner*, 3 vols. (Leipzig, 1902–8). In the preface to *Andria* Donatus calls the protasis "subtilis," the epitasis "tumultuosa," and the catastrophe "paene tragica." (1:35–36).

19. Molière, *Oeuvres complètes*, 2 vols. (Paris, 1971), All subsequent references to Molière's plays are to this edition.

20. I have taken the text from Henry Mayhew, *London Labour and the London Poor*, Vol. 3 (New York, Dover, 1968), 43–60.

21. Ibid., 57.

22. Ibid., 59.

23. Eric Bentley, in *The Life of the Drama* (New York, 1974), describes this aspect of farce, in this case the French farce of the nineteenth century. "Life is a kind of universal milling around, a rushing from bedroom to bedroom driven by demons more dreadful than sensuality . . . there is something spastic about farce generally" (247).

24. Jonson uses the phrase *Vetus comoedia* in *Every Man out of his Humour*, Grex 212, though this has been taken to mean the native comedy of the English folk tradition. See Ian Donaldson's discussion of the passage in *The World Upside-Down* (Oxford, 1970), 26n.

25. A. W. Pickard-Cambridge, in *Dithyramb, Tragedy, and Comedy* (Oxford, 1927), 211, links the victory songs of the Chorus in *The Birds, Lysistrata*, and *Ecclesiazusae* to the anticipated success of the players in the dramatic contest.

26. C. L. Barber, in *Shakespeare's Festive Comedy* (New York, 1967), points to an essential difference between revel in Aristophanes and Shakespeare. While Shakespeare has a saturnalian interest that makes his comedies like Aristophanes' celebrations of holiday (7–8), there is no clear role for saturnalia in Shakespeare's culture (239), which tended to stress the tensions between holiday and mortality.

27. Alvin B. Kernan in *The Plot of Satire* (New Haven, Conn., 1965), calls attention to the lack of development in the plots of great satires. ". . . there is little sense of any movement from one point to another. The dunces and the vicious go merrily on their way . . . the satirist stands in the foreground shouting or wryly mocking. . . . His voice is never stilled, and dullness is never converted to wisdom" (97–98).

28. Dorine, the servant in *Tartuffe*, exposes the hypocrite's claims as a future husband to Mariane in terms of a cheap provincial carnival over which Mariane would preside as Mme. Tartuffe:

> Là dans le carnaval, vous pourrez espérer
> Le bal et la grand'bande, à savoir, deux musettes,
> Et parfois Fagotin et ses marionettes.
> —*Tartuffe* (2.3.664–66)

29. Gogol in his notes to the play stresses the importance of the final tableau:

The cast should be specially attentive to the concluding tableau. The final speech from the Gendarme must stun everybody on stage, immediately and simultaneously, like an electric shock. The entire company should shift and freeze its positions in a single instant. (N. Gogol, *The Government Inspector*, trans. Edward O. Marsh and Jeremy Brooks [London, 1968], 16 n.)

30. Ibid., 2.1.

31. Molière, *Le Malade imaginaire*, 3.14. "Le carnaval autorise cela."

32. George E. Duckworth in *The Nature of Roman Comedy* (Princeton, 1971) calls the

conventional recognition scene of comedies of mistaken identity "a rather mechanical device" (p. 160). It is mechanical but it can be made to bear a certain amount of pathos as I try to show in my example from Plautus's *Captives*.

33. For some suggestive ideas on what there is in common between the world of Shakespeare's last plays and of New Comedy see Leo Salingar, *Shakespeare and the Traditions of Comedy* (Cambridge, 1974), 173–74.

34. Molière, Oeuvres complètes, vol. 2.

35. Edmund Spenser, *The Faerie Queene*, ed. J. C. Smith (Oxford, 1909), Bk. 7, Canto 8.2.

36. Ovid's *Metamorphoses, The Arthur Golding Translation, 1567*, ed. John Frederick Nims (New York, 1965), 15.270–78.

37. *The Faerie Queene*, Bk. 7, Canto 7.58.

38. Nevill Coghill, in "The Basis of Shakespearean Comedy," *Essays and Studies*, n.s., 3 (1950): 1–28, posits a different formula. Concentrating on the steps of the plot rather than on what happens to a character, he sees the essential Shakespearean comic structure as "a tale of trouble that turned into joy" (p. 4). Northrop Frye, in *A Natural Perspective* (New York, 1965), esp. chap. 4, sees the action of Shakespearean comedy as both cyclical and dialectical (p. 133). According to Frye "the renewing power of the final action lifts us into a higher world, and separates that world from the world of the comic action itself" (133). A more character-oriented definition of the cyclical action of Shakespearean comedy is in Salingar, *Shakespeare and the Traditions of Comedy*. Salingar in chap. 1 links the cycles of Fortune and Nature with the errors and loss of identity that are stages in a return to self (pp. 24–26).

39. In a completely different way the circle plot expresses the trapped condition of Bergson's comic victims. "To cover a good deal of ground only to come back unwittingly to the starting-point, is to make a great effort for a result that is nil." Henri Bergson, "Laughter," in *Comedy*, intro. Wylie Sypher (Garden City, N.Y., 1956).

CHAPTER 2

1. Lorenzo Da Ponte, *Memoirs of Lorenzo Da Ponte*, trans. Elizabeth Abbot (Philadelphia, 1929), 133.

2. In Plautus the epilogue may itself be a joke as when Daemones in *The Rope* invites the audience to dinner sixteen years later. In *Stichus*, on the other hand, the audience, having watched a bout of frenzied dancing on stage, is sent home to continue the party.

3. Meyerhold's famous Moscow production of the play provides a clear example of the theatrical viability of the deadlock-riot polarity. Nick Worrall, in "Meyerhold Directs Gogol's *Government Inspector*," *Theatre Quarterly* 2 (July–September 1972): 75–95, describes the final sequence of the play:

> As if in belated response to the mayor's cry about his disgrace being "sounded from the steeples," the town bells suddenly began to ring out. The noise increased as the policemen began beating drums and blowing whistles. Underneath the cacophonous din, the Jewish orchestra could be heard playing a dance melody. Accompanying the din with their own shrieks and wails of horror, the entire cast cavorted and pranced across the open stage with their hands linked together, in a snaking, dancing file led by a fiddler. They looked like figures in a medieval Dance of Death. Across the stage they danced and through the lighted auditorium; into a medieval market place.
> As the sound of their exit died away, the clanging and the drumming stopped, and in the dead silence which followed, a white curtain began to rise slowly upwards out of the orchestra pit, until it completely obscured the stage. On it were the words: "A

Government Inspector, appointed by Imperial Decree, has arrived from St. Petersburg. He is waiting at the inn and requires your presence there immediately." The curtain continued upwards and disappeared.

In the middle of the hitherto empty stage, and forming a half circle across its width, were fully clothed, life-size dummies, every one of which was a replica of a character in the play. They stood as if caught in a moment of life, mostly in grotesque attitudes, standing, kneeling, gesturing, grimacing. It was as if Death had come to each, unexpectedly, as he might to victims of a volcano disaster just unchipped from a preserving mould of lava.

It was already five minutes after midnight but the audience, instead of hurrying away, sat motionlessly in the lighted auditorium, as they contemplated the spectacle of grotesque effigies. They watched for at least the full minute and a half, which Gogol asks that they should, and even longer. In achieving this alone, Meyerhold had stagemanaged a minor miracle. (94)

CHAPTER 3

1. Jonson gives trenchant expression to his moral aims in the dedicatory epistle to *Volpone.* See Ben Jonson, *Works,* ed. C. H. Herford and P. and E. Simpson (Oxford, 1925–52), vol. 5. All quotations from Jonson are from this text.

2. Gabriele Bernhard Jackson, in *Vision and Judgment in Jonson's Drama* (New Haven, Conn., 1968), wrongly claims, it seems to me, that most of Jonson's plays end with an arrangement of society in which the best person is most highly valued (69). She sees chaos and uncontrolled passion as precursors of final stability in Jonson's comedy (93). In my view the pattern is more artistic than moral.

3. I discuss the epilogues in my analysis of these plays below.

4. Dryden, *Essays,* 1:83–89.

5. T. S. Eliot, *Elizabethan Dramatists* (London, 1963), 76. The essay on Ben Jonson dates from 1919.

6. Ray L. Heffner, Jr., "Unifying Symbols in the Comedy of Ben Jonson," in *English Stage Comedy,* ed. W. K. Wimsatt, Jr. (New York, 1954), 74–97. Donaldson, *The World Upside-Down,* chaps. 2 and 3.

7. Erasmus, *The Praise of Folly,* trans. Hoyt Hopewell Hudson (Princeton, N.J., 1941), 37.

8. Edgar C. Knowlton, in "The Plots of Ben Jonson," *Modern Language Notes* 44 (1929): 77–86, attempts to show that the false ending of act 4 is characteristic of Jonson's comedy. He finds that act 4 sets up a solution that was "often unsatisfactory to the moral taste of the audience and was intended to be so" (79). In terms of the rhetorical criticism of Donatus and Scaliger, this false solution would be the epitasis or catastasis *(vigor ac status fabulae).*

9. The ending of *Volpone* perplexed Dryden *(Essays* I, 73), who finds two actions in the play, one ending in act 4 and the other beginning in act 5. To justify this, Dryden, or his spokesman Neander, posits two characters of Volpone; one a cunning person and the other a voluptuary. His contemporary Dennis also found Volpone's behavior inconsistent. In a letter to Congreve (Jonson, *Works,* 11:555) he calls Volpone (in act 5) a "Giddy Coxcombe, in the Conduct of that very Affair which he manag'd so craftily in the first four."

10. John Creaser in *"Volpone:* The Mortifying of the Fox," *Essays in Criticism* 25 (1975): 329–56, finds a theatrical gaiety and ingenuity in Volpone's very act of self-destruction. He argues rightly against taking Jonson's claim to rigor (in the *Epistle)* at its face value. I think he goes too far, and maintain that there is a difference between the theatricality of Volpone's discovery to Celia and his forced unmasking before the Avocatori.

11. Mark A. Anderson, "Structure and Response in *Volpone*," *Renaissance and Modern Studies* 19 (1975): 47–71, is overstating the subversive effect of the epilogue. He claims that it is Volpone and not an actor who comes forward to ask our approval, thereby exposing the audience (70). This seems wrong because the epilogue always occupies the middle ground between the completed illusion (the play) and the display of art (the actor's and the poet's).

12. Ian Donaldson, "*Volpone:* Quick and Dead," *Essays in Criticism* 21 (1971): 121–34, is right when he finds that in looking at Jonson's statement of intent in the *Epistle* "there is nothing in this account to prepare us for the buoyant and mischievous comic energies of the play itself" (121).

13. Judd Arnold, "Lovewit's Triumph and Jonsonian Morality: A Reading of *The Alchemist*," *Criticism* 11 (1969): 151–66, argues that Face is exposed at the end (162). He finds sarcasm in Lovewit's speech of tribute to Jeremy (5.5.146–52). I think the speech is ironic about masters and servants and their relationship but not at the expense of the servant.

14. Paul Goodman in a perceptive essay on comic plots, *The Structure of Literature* (Chicago, 1962), chap. 3, makes much of the return to normality with Lovewit's appearance. He could well have included *The Alchemist* in his group of comedies like *The Acharnians*, which end without deflation and therefore have a "peculiar heady glory" (88).

15. Jackson, *Vision and Judgment in Jonson's Drama* understands pattern in an exclusively moral sense. Thus she finds that "the inability to establish a valid final pattern is the most telling judgment this society makes on itself" (69). However, the perfect pattern of a trickster comedy is disarmingly amoral, a tribute to art and wit, a judgment of folly more than of knavery.

16. Edward Partridge, *The Broken Compass* (New York, 1958), finds a sinister note in Face's epilogue (pp. 154–55). Partridge suggests that Face, putting himself on the spectators as his "countrey," implies that they are more stuff to be exploited.

17. On Truewit's neutrality see John J. Enck, *Jonson and the Comic Truth* (Madison, Wis., 1957), 143.

18. See Jonas A. Barish, *Ben Jonson and the Language of Prose Comedy* (Cambridge, Mass., 1967), 157: "Morose, on the other hand, is always himself."

19. Ibid., 182, notes that the likening of living things to blocks of stone and metal artifacts corresponds to a "a certain frigidity at the heart of the play."

20. For a survey of carnival practices in a literary context see Mikhail Bakhtin, *Rabelais and His World,* trans. Hélène Iswolsky (Cambridge, Mass., and London, 1968), chaps. 3 and 4.

21. Goethe, *Italian Journey*, trans. W. H. Auden and Elizabeth Mayer (Harmondsworth, England, 1970) 468–69.

22. For a discussion of the way the characters are separated and put into surprising roles and combinations by the fair, see Richard Levin, "The Structure of *Bartholomew Fair*," *PMLA* 80 (1965): 172–79.

23. Jonson, *Works,* 9:245.

24. I am indebted in my discussion to Ian Donaldson's notion of the importance of *license* in the play. See *The World Upside-Down,* 50–58.

25. The symbolic use of *warrant* is discussed by Heffner, "Unifying Symbols," 142–46.

26. Compare Jonson's Epigram 75, *On Lippe, the Teacher:*

> I Cannot thinke there's that antipathy
> 'Twixt *puritanes,* and *players,* as some cry;

Though LIPPE, at PAULS, ranne from his text away,
T'inveigh 'gainst playes: what did he then but play?
(Works, 8:52).

CHAPTER 4

1. Jacques Scherer, in *La Dramaturgie classique en France* (Paris, 1962), defines the aim of denouement in seventeenth-century practice thus: "Il faut que le sort de tous les personnages importants soit fixé et qu'aucun des problèmes posés par la pièce ne reste sans solution" (128). Formally this is true of Molière's endings but the formal artifice of conclusion often begs the question of change.

2. Georges Poulet, in *Studies in Human Time*, trans. Elliot Colemen (Baltimore, Md., 1956), 102, writes memorably of the "essentially repetitive process by which Molière's characters continually manifest themselves." He finds this pattern a cycle of triumphant and frustrated passion, and essentially tragic.

3. This was noticed by Gustave Lanson in his famous article, "Molière et la farce," originally in *Revue de Paris* (1901), 129–53, reprinted in Lanson, *Essais de méthode, de critique et d'histoire littéraire*, ed. Henri Peyre (Paris, 1965), 190–210. For Lanson the permanence of the mask makes denouement impossible without external artifice. Molière's characters "doivent être tels à la fin qu'au début . . ." (207).

4. I follow the Pléiade editor in counting these farces as part of Molière's oeuvre. See Molière, *Oeuvres complètes*, 1:6.

5. Lanson, *Essais de méthode*, laid the foundation for the study of Molière by way of farce. "L'origine de la comédie de Molière, de toute cette comédie, jusqu'en ces plus hautes manifestations . . . doit être cherchée dans la farce" (191–92).

6. J. D. Hubert in *Molière and the Comedy of Intellect* (Berkeley, Calif., and London, 1962), finds that Scapin "seems to improvise the action like a character from the *Commedia dell'Arte*" (233).

7. When the play was first presented at Versailles before Louis (1668), each act was preceded and followed by an elaborate spectacle of pastoral song and dance. Thus Dandin's provincial grossness was offset by a more polite and flattering kind of entertainment, in which the dances turn Dandin's thoughts of suicide into the consolations of wine. He then becomes a reluctant spectator of the ballet.

8. This is not to say that the aristocratic audience at Versailles was not thoroughly amused by Dandin's plight.

9. A summary of the controversy can be found in Jacques Scherer, *Structures de "Tartuffe,"* (Paris, 1966), 190–96. See also G. Michaut, *Les Luttes de Molière* (Geneva, 1968), 55–56. Michaut quotes the hostile *Lettre satirique sur le Tartuffe* on the denouement: "il tranche le noeud qu'il n'a su dénouer."

10. *Lettre* in Molière, *Oeuvres complètes*, 1:1168.

11. Ibid., 1168.

12. Ibid.

13. *Correspondance entre Boileau-Despréaux et Brossette*, ed. Auguste Laverdet (Paris, 1858), 516.

14. Ibid.

15. Michaut, *Luttes de Molière*, 64–65, believes that the first version of the play performed at Versailles in 1664 ended after three acts with the hypocrite triumphant. The Pléiade editor does not reject this reconstruction; see Molière, *Oeuvres complètes*, 1:834–35.

16. See F. Brunetière, *Les Époques du Théâtre Français, 1656–1850* (Paris, 1896),

138: "Il y a des vices pour Molière, dont le rire du parterre ne saurait suffire à faire justice."

17. *Lettre,* in Molière, *Oeuvres complètes,* 1:1152. The writer says Orgon's infatuation is necessary "afin que le changement qui se fera dans lui quand il sera désabusé (qui est proprement le sujet de la pièce) paraisse d'autant plus merveilleux au spectateur."

18. Jacques Guicharnaud, in *Molière, une aventure théâtrale* (Paris, 1963), makes the point succinctly. "Aussi la comédie moliéresque ne comporte-t-elle pas de solution 'de l'intérieur' des héros. La solution est offerte par des conventions du genre, des effets purement scéniques ou des besoins d'équilibre formel" (p. 41). In the case of Orgon, Guicharnaud distinguishes between the brutal enlightenment of the character, which takes place, and change, which does not (41).

19. This pattern of repeated failure and contretemps has been described by René Bray, in *Molière, homme de théâtre* (Paris, 1954), 206, as being the rhythmic basis of the action.

20. Jacques Copeau, *Molière* (Paris, 1976), 223–24: "En un mot, le mouvement de la comédie n'est qu'une projection du mouvement du caractère."

21. The parallel is drawn unequivocally by René Jasinski in *Molière et Le Misanthrope* (Paris, 1951), 145. Jasinski points out that like Dandin, Alceste's defeat is sought out by himself: " 'Tu l'as voulu, Alceste,' lui dirait-on volontiers, comme à George Dandin."

22. Guicharnaud, *Molière,* points to the pure Racinian classicism of structure in both *Le Misanthrope* and *George Dandin.* Both comedies, he says (495), open with characters on the verge of an all-important decision and enact the progress towards it. Jasinski, *Molière Le Misanthrope,* 281, also makes a Racinian comparison (to *Bérénice*) on the basis of the trap situation and the economy of means employed to bring it to its crisis.

23. Molière, *Oeuvres complètes,* 2:139.

24. Guicharnaud, *Molière,* draws attention to the significance of the empty stage at the end as an image of isolation and defeat (498).

25. André Gide, *Journals 1889–1949,* trans. J. O'Brien (Harmondsworth, 1967), 671.

26. I differ here with W. G. Moore, *Molière, a New Criticism* (Oxford, 1949), who makes no distinction between the imprisoning dance of *L'Amour médecin* and the tolerant carnival of *Le Malade imaginaire* in his brief reference to ceremony and dance at the end of Molière's plays (p.84).

CHAPTER 5

1. See my discussion in chapter 1 of the Ovidian and Spenserian cycles as pagan and Christian ways of encountering change.

2. My quotations from Shakespeare are all from William Shakespeare, *The Riverside Shakespeare,* Textual Editor G. Blakemore Evans et al. (Boston, 1978).

3. Dr. Johnson found evidence of neglect and haste in Shakespeare's catastrophes in general. Johnson attributed this hurry, characteristically, to the poet's desire to pocket up his wages and have done. See his "Preface" in *Johnson on Shakespeare,* ed. Arthur Sherbo, *The Yale Edition of the Works of Samuel Johnson* (New Haven, Conn., and London, 1968), 7:71–72.

4. T. W. Baldwin, in *Shakspere's Five-Act Structure* (Urbana, Ill., 1947), ch. 29, stresses Shakespeare's use of the five-act division found in sixteenth-century editions of Plautus (700). Baldwin's interest in the influence of the Roman model on Shakespeare blinds him to the differences in mood and in comic shape.

5. This pattern, an integrating structure of a totally different kind from that of Baldwin, is thus described by Ralph Berry, *Shakespeare's Comedies* (Princeton, N.J., 1972), 26: "The structural idea of *The Comedy of Errors* I apprehend to be the union of two halves, each seeking the other, paralleling and complementing the other, ultimately to be reconciled."

6. Alexander Leggatt, *Shakespeare's Comedy of Love* (London, 1974), seems to me to be wrong to diminish the importance of Egeon's story (14–15). The narration may be rhetorical and literary but it is the frame that accentuates the shape of the action.

7. That a formal structure is shared by *The Comedy of Errors* and *The Tempest* is noticed by Frank Kermode in the Introduction to *The Tempest*, New Arden edition (London, 1962), lxxiv–lxxv.

8. See Douglas L. Peterson's description of the action as "emblematic narrative" in *Time, Tide and Tempest* (San Marino, Calif., 1973), 217. Peterson emphasizes the correspondences and parallels that move the action forward rather than the narrative sequence, which I stress.

9. Criticism has mostly dwelt on the absurdities, to a modern taste, of the device. A. P. Rossiter, for instance, in *Angel with Horns* (London, 1961), 125, says that the "inquiringness" of the problem comedies makes for a tension between the device itself and our curiosity about the minds of those who take part in it. Critics with a more historical bias like W. W. Lawrence in *Shakespeare's Problem Comedies* (London, 1969), find the device's acceptability in its currency: "they were current in the storytelling of his own day" (p. 97). Studies of the thematic relevance of the device are less common, but see James Black, "The Unfolding of *Measure for Measure*," *Shakespeare Survey* 26 (1973): 119–28.

10. In an enlightening article, Ian Donaldson ("*All's Well That Ends Well:* Shakespeare's Play of Endings," *Essays in Criticism* 27 [1977]: 34–55), analyzes the thematic use of different conceptions of *end* and *ending* in the play. He does not focus, as I do, on the act of exchange, which makes a good ending of a bad intent.

11. For example, G. K. Hunter in the introduction to the New Arden edition of the play (1967), pp. xlvi–xlvii, who finds Bertram a success on the level of Jonsonian caricature but incoherent on any deeper level.

12. Lawrence, *Shakespeare's Problem Comedies*, 78.

13. Samuel Johnson, *Johnson on Shakespeare*, 7:400.

14. William Painter, *The Palace of Pleasure*, Novel 38 in Geoffrey Bullough, *Narrative and Dramatic Sources of Shakespeare*, vol. 2 (London and New York, 1958). The relevant passage is on p. 396.

15. J. L. Calderwood, "Styles of Knowing in *All's Well*," *Modern Language Quarterly* 25 (1964): 293.

16. James Black in "The Unfolding of *Measure for Measure*," is one of the few critics who take seriously the device of substitution, especially Mariana's for Isabella. See 124–26.

17. See Ernest Schanzer, *The Problem Plays of Shakespeare* (New York, 1965), 100. Schanzer quotes, though he does not agree with, Quiller-Couch's view that Isabel and Angelo are "two pendent portraits or studies in the ugliness of Puritan hypocrisy" (105).

18. See Bertrand Evans's subtle analysis of this awareness in *Shakespeare's Comedies* (Oxford, 1960), 209. Evans describes Angelo as "a figure at once odious, comic and pathetic: supposing himself guilty of heinous crimes of which remembrance tortures him, but which he is convinced he can keep hidden, he is truly guilty of no criminal acts, but all his intents are known to the authority who can call him to account."

19. Mary Lascelles, in *Shakespeare's "Measure for Measure"* (London, 1953), 157, makes the point succinctly: "To will, and to do harm are, according to the logic of Shakespearean tragi-comedy, distinct."

20. Baldwin, *Shakspere's Five-Act Structure*, 715–16, stresses the Terentian model of construction that, he claims, underlies both *The Comedy of Errors* and *Twelfth Night*.

21. For a study of this frustration as it is projected through the device of the message see Berry, *Shakespeare's Comedies,* 196–211.

22. John Russell Brown, in his essay "The Presentation of Comedy: The First Ten Plays," in *Shakespearean Comedy,* ed. J. R. Brown and B. Harris, Stratford-upon-Avon Studies, vol. 14 (London, 1972), 9–30, notices that Viola has only a "silent approach to Orsino" at the end and "this must serve to sum up all her performance" (p. 28).

23. Yet one hesitates to accept such a bluntly positive position as Larry S. Champion's in *The Evolution of Shakespeare's Comedy* (Cambridge, Mass., 1970), 94: "They have faced the therapy of exposure, have been laughed from their abnormal postures, and, presumably, have every reason to expect a richer and more productive life as a consequence of their self-knowledge."

24. Evans, *Shakespeare's Comedies,* 311, says that the references to the impossibility of resurrecting Hermione at the beginning of act 5 suggest that Shakespeare "aims to make amends for the bad treatment given our awareness in earlier acts."

25. Sir Arthur Quiller-Couch in his introduction to *The Winter's Tale,* ed. A. Quiller-Couch and J. Dover Wilson (Cambridge, 1950), xxiii.

26. Neville Coghill, "Six Points of Stage-Craft in *The Winter's Tale,*" *Shakespeare Survey* 11 (1958): 39.

27. William H. Matchett, "Some Dramatic Techniques in *The Winter's Tale,*" *Shakespeare Survey* 22 (1969): 103.

Select Bibliography

Anderson, Mark A. "Structure and Response in *Volpone.*" *Renaissance and Modern Studies* 19 (1975): 47–71.

Aristophanes. Translated by B. B. Rogers. 3 vols. Loeb Classical Library. 1924. Reprint. London and Cambridge, Mass.; Harvard University Press, 1967.

Arnold, Judd. "Lovewit's Triumph and Jonsonian Morality: A Reading of *The Alchemist.*" *Criticism* 11 (1969): 151–66.

Bakhtin, Mikhail. *Rabelais and His World.* Translated by Hélène Iswoisky. Cambridge, Mass., and London: Harvard University Press, 1968.

Baldwin, T. W. *Shakspere's Five-Act Structure.* Urbana: University of Illinois Press, 1947.

Barber, C. L. *Shakespeare's Festive Comedy.* New York: Meridian, 1967.

Barish, Jonas A. *Ben Jonson and the Language of Prose Comedy.* Cambridge, Mass.: Harvard University Press, 1967.

Baudelaire, Charles. *Ecrits sur l'Art.* 2 vols. Paris: Livre de Poche, 1971.

Bentley, Eric. *The Life of the Drama.* New York: Atheneum, 1964.

Bergson, Henri. "Laughter." In *Comedy,* introduction by Wylie Sypher. Garden City, N.Y.: Doubleday, 1956.

Berry, Ralph. *Shakespeare's Comedies.* Princeton, N.J.: Princeton University Press, 1972.

Black, James. "The Unfolding of *Measure for Measure.*" *Shakespeare Survey* 26 (1973): 119–28.

Boileau-Despréaux et Brossette, Correpondance entre. Edited by Auguste Laverdet. Paris: J. Techener, Libraire, 1858.

Bray, René. *Molière, homme de théâtre.* Paris: Mercure de France, 1954.

Brown, John Russell. "The Presentation of Comedy: The First Ten Plays." In *Shakespearean Comedy,* edited by J. R. Brown and B. Harris, 9–30. Stratford-upon-Avon Studies, vol. 14. London: E. Arnold, 1972.

Brunetière, F. *Les Époques du théâtre Français, 1656–1850.* Paris, 1896.

Bullough, Geoffrey, ed. *Narrative and Dramatic Sources of Shakespeare.* 8 vols. London and New York: Columbia University Press, 1957–75.

Butcher, S. H. *Aristotle's Theory of Poetry and Fine Art.* London: MacMillan & Co., 1911.

Calderwood, J. L. "Styles of Knowing in *All's Well.*" *Modern Language Quarterly* 25 (1964): 272–94.

Champion, Larry S. *The Evolution of Shakespeare's Comedy*. Cambridge, Mass.: Harvard University Press, 1970.

Coghill, Neville. "The Basis of Shakespearean Comedy." *Essays and Studies*, n.s. 3 (1950): 1–28.

———. "Six Points of Stage-Craft in *The Winter's Tale*," *Shakespeare Survey* 11 (1958): 31–41.

Copeau, Jacques. *Molière*. Paris: Gallimard, 1976.

Creaser, John. "*Volpone:* The Mortifying of the Fox." *Essays in Criticism* 25 (1975): 329–56.

Da Ponte, Lorenzo. *Memoirs of Lorenzo Da Ponte*. Translated by Elizabeth Abbott. Philadelphia: J. B. Lippincott & Co., 1929.

Donaldson, Ian. "*All's Well That Ends Well:* Shakespeare's Play of Endings." *Essays in Criticism* 27 (1977): 34–55.

———. "*Volpone:* Quick and Dead." *Essays in Criticism* 21 (1971): 121–34.

———. *The World Upside-Down: Comedy from Jonson to Fielding*. Oxford: At the University Press, 1970.

Donatus, Aelius. *Aeli Donati quod fertur commentum Terenti*. Edited by Paul Wessner, 3 vols. Leipzig, 1902–8.

Doran, Madeleine. *Endeavors of Art:* A Study of Form in Elizabethan Drama. Madison: University of Wisconsin Press, 1964.

Dryden, John. *Essays*. Edited by W. P. Ker. 2 vols. Oxford: At the Clarendon Press, 1926.

Duckworth, George E. *The Nature of Roman Comedy*. Princeton, N.J.: Princeton University Press, 1971.

Eliot, T. S. *Elizabethan Dramatists*. London: Faber and Faber, 1963.

Enck, John J. *Jonson and the Comic Truth*. Madison: University of Wisconsin Press, 1957.

Erasmus. *The Praise of Folly*. Translated by Hoyt Hopewell Hudson. Princeton, N.J.: Princeton University Press, 1941.

Evans, Bertrand. *Shakespeare's Comedies*. Oxford: At the University Press, 1960.

Frye, Northrop. *Anatomy of Criticism* Princeton, N.J.: Princeton University Press, 1971.

———. *A Natural Perspective*. New York: Columbia University Press, 1965.

Gay, John. *The Beggar's Opera*. Edited by John Hampden. London: Everyman, 1964.

Gide, André. *Journals 1889–1949*. Translated by J. O'Brien. Harmondsworth: Penguin, 1967.

Goethe, Wolfgang. *Italian Journey*. Translated by W. H. Auden and Elizabeth Mayer. Harmondsworth, England: Penguin Books, 1970.

Gogol, Nikolai. *The Government Inspector*. Translated by Edward O. Marsh and Jeremy Brooks. London: Methuen, 1968.

Goodman, Paul. *The Structure of Literature*. Chicago: University of Chicago Press, 1962.

Guicharnaud, Jacques. *Molière, une aventure théâtrale*. Paris: Gallimard, 1963.

Heffner, Ray L., Jr. "Unifying Symbols in the Comedy of Ben Jonson." In *English Stage Comedy*, edited by W. K. Wimsatt, Jr., 74–97. New York: Columbia University Press, 1954.

Herrick, Marvin T. *Comic Theory in the Sixteenth Century*. Urbana: University of Illinois Press, 1964.

Herrnstein Smith, Barbara. *Poetic Closure: A Study of How Poems End*. Chicago: University of Chicago Press, 1968.

Horace. *Satires, Epistles and Ars Poetica*. Translated by H. Rushton Fairclough. Loeb Classics. London and Cambridge, Mass.: Harvard University Press, 1942.

Hubert, J. D. *Molière and the Comedy of Intellect*. Berkeley and London: University of California Press, 1962.

Jackson, Gabriele Bernhard. *Vision and Judgment in Jonson's Drama*. New Haven, Conn.: Yale University Press, 1968.

Jasinski, René. *Molière et Le Misanthrope*. Paris: Colin, 1951.

Johnson, Samuel. *Johnson on Shakespeare*. Edited by Arthur Sherbo. Vols. 7 and 8 of *The Yale Edition of the Works of Samuel Johnson*. New Haven, Conn., and London, 1958–1971.

Jonson, Ben. *Works*. Edited by C. H. Herford and P. and E. Simpson. 11 vols. Oxford: At the University Press, 1925–52.

Kernan, Alvin B. *The Plot of Satire*. New Haven, Conn.: Yale University Press, 1965.

Knowlton, Edgar C. "The Plots of Ben Jonson." *Modern Language Notes* 44 (1929): 77–86.

Lanson, Gustave. *Essais de méthode, de critique et d'histoire littéraire*. Edited by Henri Peyre. Paris: Hachette, 1965.

Lascelles, Mary. *Shakespeare's "Measure for Measure."* London: Athlone Press, 1953.

Lawrence, W. W. *Shakespeare's Problem Comedies*. Harmondsworth: Penguin Shakespeare Library, 1969.

Leggatt, Alexander. *Shakespeare's Comedy of Love*. London: Methuen, 1974.

Levin, Richard. "The Structure of *Bartholomew Fair*." *PMLA* 80 (1965): 172–79.

Matchett, William H. "Some Dramatic Techniques in *The Winter's Tale*." *Shakespeare Survey* 22 (1969): 93–107.

Mayhew, Henry. *London Labour and the London Poor*. New York, Dover, 1968.

Michaut, G. *Les Luttes de Molière*. Geneva: Slatkine Reprints, 1968.

Molière. *Oeuvres complètes*. 2 vols. Paris: Bibliothèque de la Pléiade, 1971.

Moore, W. G. *Molière, a New Criticism*. Oxford: Clarendon Press, 1949.

Olson, Elder. *The Theory of Comedy*. Bloomington: Indiana University Press, 1968.

Ovid. *Metamorphoses. The Arthur Golding Translation, 1567.* Edited by John Frederick Nims. New York: Macmillan, 1965.

Partridge, Edward. *The Broken Compass: A Study of the Major Comedies of Ben Jonson.* New York: Columbia University Press, 1968.

Peterson, Douglas L. *Time, Tide and Tempest: A Study of Shakespeare's Romances.* San Marino, Calif: Huntington Library Publications, 1973.

Pickard-Cambridge, A. W. *Dithyramb, Tragedy, and Comedy.* Oxford: At the University Press, 1927.

Plato. *The Dialogues.* Translated by B. Jowett. 5 vols. Oxford, 1892.

Plautus. Translated by Paul Nixon. 5 vols. Loeb Classical Library. 1916, Reprint. London and Cambridge, Mass.: Harvard University Press, 1966.

Poulet, Georges. *Studies in Human Time.* Translated by Elliot Coleman. Baltimore, Md.: Johns Hopkins University Press, 1956.

Rossiter, A. P. *Angel with Horns,* London: Longman, 1961.

Salingar, Leo. *Shakespeare and the Traditions of Comedy.* Cambridge: At the University Press, 1974.

Schanzer, Ernest. *The Problem Plays of Shakespeare.* New York: Schocken, 1965.

Scherer, Jacques. *La Dramaturgie classique en France.* Paris: Nizet, 1962.

―――. *Structures de "Tartuffe."* Paris: Société d'édition d'enseignement supérieur, 1966.

Shakespeare, William. *The Riverside Shakespeare.* Textual Editor, G. Blakemore Evans et al. Boston: Houghton Mifflin, 1978.

―――. *All's Well That Ends Well.* Edited by G. K. Hunter. New Arden Edition. London: Methuen, 1967.

―――. *The Tempest.* Edited by Frank Kermode. New Arden Edition. London: Methuen, 1962.

―――. *The Winter's Tale.* Edited by Sir Arthur Quiller-Couch and J. Dover Wilson. Cambridge: At the University Press, 1950.

Sidney, Sir Philip. *Works.* Edited by W. Gray. London, 1893.

Spenser, Edmund. *The Poetical Works.* Edited by Ernest De Selincourt and J. C. Smith. 3 vols. Oxford, 1909–10.

Terence. Translated by John Sargeaunt. 2 vols. Loeb Classical Library. London and New York, 1912.

Worrall, Nick. "Meyerhold Directs Gogol's *Government Inspector.*" *Theatre Quarterly* 2 (July–September 1972): 75–95.

Index

Anderson, Mark A., 166n
Aristophanes: *The Acharnians*, 23; *The Birds*, 23; *The Clouds*, 17, 23; *Lysistrata*, 16, 23, 24
Aristotle, 12–13, 16, 18–19, 20
Arnold, Judd, 166n

Bakhtin, Mikhail, 166n
Baldwin, T. W., 168n, 170n
Barber, C. L., 163n
Barish, Jonas A., 166n
Baudelaire, Charles, 162
Beggar's Opera, The, 14
Bentley, Eric, 163n
Bergson, Henri, 164n
Berry, Ralph, 169n, 170n
Black, James, 169n
Boileau, Nicolas, 93, 94
Bray, René, 168n
Brossette, Claude, 93
Brown, John Russell, 170n

Calderwood, J. L., 131
Carnival: described by Goethe, 67–68; by Horace, 14; in Jonson, 68–77; in Molière, 108–110
Champion, Larry S., 170n
Clair, René, 22
Coghill, Neville, 159, 164n
Coleridge, S. T., 51
Copeau, Jacques, 100
Creaser, John, 165n

Da Ponte, Lorenzo, 33–34, 41, 57, 59
Deadlock, 17; in *Epicoene*, 64–65; in Molière, 79, 82, 90, 92, 101; in *Twelfth Night*, 151. *See also Riot*
Denouement, 18, 20; in farce and satire, 22, 23, 25; in Molière, 78–110

Discovery: in farce, 22; in Jonson, 53–56, 58, 72–73, 76–77; in Molière, 79–80, 84–87, 89–92, 96–100, 101–2, 105–6; in Roman comedy, 28; in Shakespearean comedy, 30, 121, 134–36; and unmasking, 37
Dominion of Fancy, The (Punch's play), 21
Donaldson, Ian, 45, 163n, 166n, 169n
Donatus, 18–19
Donneau de Visé, Jean, 106
Dryden, John, 165n; *An Essay of Dramatic Poesy*, 17, 18, 29, 44
Duckworth, George, E., 163–64n

Eliot, T. S., 45
Enck, John J., 166n
Ending devices: epilogue, 35, 44, 51, 70, 119; finale, 33–34, 57, 59; play-within-the-play, 35–36, 62, 73–76; repetition, 38–39; tableau, 12, 39–42, 108; trial, 36–37, 123; unmasking, 37–38, 50, 59–64, 137–43. *See also* Denouement; Discovery; Recognition
Erasmus, 46
Evans, Bertrand, 159, 169n, 170n

Farce, 20, 22, 23, 25, 27, 28, 38, 39, 42, 80–81, 83, 117
Frye, Northrop, 162n

Gide, André, 109
Goethe, Johann Wolfgang von: *Italian Journey*, 67–68
Gogol, Nikolai: *The Government Inspector*, 25, 26, 41, 59, 117, 163n, 164–65n
Goodman, Paul, 166n
Guicharnaud, Jacques, 168n

Heffner, Ray L. Jr., 45

175

Herrick, Marvin T., 162n
Herrnstein Smith, Barbara, 162n
Horace, 14
Hubert, J. D., 167n
Hunter, G. K., 169n

Italian Straw Hat, An, 22, 29, 31

Jackson, Gabriele Bernhard, 165n, 166n
Jasinski, René, 168n
Johnson, Samuel, 130
Jonson, Ben, 17, 23, 35, 38, 43, 44–77, 78,
   86, 88, 97, 110, 111, 161. *Works: The Al-*
   chemist, 26, 27, 39, 41, 44, 45, 46, 47, 51–
   59, 60, 66, 88, 97; *Bartholomew Fair,* 35,
   38, 44, 47, 48, 67–77, 79, 110; *Dis-*
   coveries, 46–47; *Epicoene,* 37, 44, 45, 46,
   59–66, 79, 88, 111, 154; *Every Man out of*
   His Humour, 25, 48; *The Magnetic Lady,*
   45; *Volpone,* 16, 17, 37, 44, 45, 47, 48–51,
   59, 66, 79, 97, 111
Juvenal, 25

Keaton, Buster (in *The General*), 38
Kermode, Frank, 169n
Kernan, Alvin B., 163n
Knowlton, Edgar C., 165n

Lascelles, Mary, 170n
Lawrence, W. W., 130, 169n
Leggatt, Alexander, 169n
Lettre sur la comédie de l'Imposteur, 93, 95
Levin, Richard, 166n

Marlowe, Christopher, 50
Marx Brothers, The, 22
Matchett, William, 160
Mayhew, Henry, 21
Michaut, G., 167n
Molière, J. B. P., 17, 19, 20, 23, 27, 28,
   42, 43, 78–110, 111, 113, 161; *Works:*
   L'Amour médecin, 110; *Le Bourgeois*
   gentilhomme, 27, 36, 38, 107; *La Critique*
   de l'École des femmes, 29, 56, 78, 80, 87,
   89, 91; *L'École des femmes,* 78, 79, 80,
   87–93, 111; *Les Fourberies de Scapin,*
   78, 79, 81–82; *George Dandin,* 38, 79, 80,
   82, 83–87, 96, 100; *La Jalousie du Bar-*
   bouillé, 80, 82–83; *Le Malade im-*
   aginaire, 21, 27, 36, 38, 80, 107–110, 111;

Le Médecin volant, 19, 80–83, 89; *Le*
   Misanthrope, 42, 78, 100–107; *Tartuffe,*
   16, 25, 79, 80, 93–100
Moore, W. G., 168n
Mozart, 34

Night at the Opera, A, 22

Old Comedy, 23–24
Ovid, 31–32

Painter, William, 130
Partridge, Edward, 166n
Peterson, Douglas, L., 169n
Pickard-Cambridge, A. W., 163n
Plato, 14–15
Plautus, 28, 34, 114, 164n; *The Braggart*
   Soldier, 34; *The Captives,* 28, 124; *The*
   Menaechmi, 22, 114, 116, 123; *The*
   Rope, 164n
Pope, Alexander, 25, 48
Poulet, Georges, 167n
Punch, 14, 21, 48, 51

Recognition, 20; and awakening, 130; and
   change, 27–30, 111, 118; and repetition,
   39, 108; in *Twelfth Night,* 149, 151–55;
   and unmasking, 38; in *The Winter's Tale,*
   159–60
Riot, 17; in *The Alchemist,* 53; in *Bar-*
   tholomew Fair, 74; contrasted with deadlock, 19–30; in *L'École des femmes,* 90–
   92
Rossiter, A. P., 169n

Salinger, Leo, 164n
Satire, 24–27, 28, 38, 39, 41, 48, 94
Schanzer, Ernest, 169n
Scherer, Jacques, 167n
Shakespeare, William, 17, 19, 20, 28–29;
   30–32, 35, 43, 46, 79; *Works: All's Well*
   That Ends Well, 30, 37, 113, 123, 127–31;
   134; *As You Like It,* 37, 40, 137, 138, 143–
   48, 150; *The Comedy of Errors,* 17, 19,
   20, 24, 30, 37, 51, 88, 91, 112, 114–18,
   123, 145, 149; *Cymbeline,* 30, 155; *Mea-*
   sure for Measure, 30, 37, 38, 123, 132–37;
   156; *The Merchant of Venice,* 30, 39, 40,
   123, 124–27, 131, 134; *A Midsummer*
   Night's Dream, 19, 20, 24, 30, 36, 54, 62,

73, 112, 129, 143, 145, 150; *Much Ado about Nothing,* 137, 138–43, 149, 155, 156; *The Tempest,* 30, 36, 39, 79, 112, 118–23, 155; *Troilus and Cressida,* 25; *Twelfth Night,* 16, 17, 33, 37, 40, 62, 65, 112, 113, 137, 138, 148–55, 157; *The Winter's Tale,* 36, 112, 137, 155–61; *Pericles,* 155

Sidney, Sir Philip, 15, 16
Spenser, Edmund, 31–32

Terence, 18; *Phormio,* 29; *The Woman of Andros,* 124
Tragedy, 13, 15, 42, 137

Worrall, Nick, 164n